THE STAMP OF INNOCENCE

THE STAMP OF INNOCENCE

THE INSPIRATIONAL STORY OF NOEL AND SIAN THOMAS

ALED GWYN JÔB

Troubador Publishing Ltd
Unit E2 Airfield Business Park,
Harrison Road, Market Harborough,
Leicestershire LE16 7UL
Tel: 0116 279 2299
Email: books@troubador.co.uk
Web: www.troubador.co.uk

ISBN 978 1 80514 302 4

British Library Cataloguing in Publication Data.
A catalogue record for this book is available from the British Library.

Printed and bound in Great Britain by 4edge Limited
Typeset in 10.5pt Minion Pro by Troubador Publishing Ltd, Leicester, UK

In loving memory of a precious son, Arfon.

The ghostwriter of *The Stamp of Innocence* is Aled Gwyn Jôb of Ynys Môn.

Aled Gwyn Jôb writes in both Welsh and English and this is his fifth published book.

Aled also writes on Twitter/X under his brand name
A Way With Words Cymru.

He also has a website under the same brand name.

Contents

Foreword

Most people by now will have heard about the Post Office scandal. A twenty-year story in which hundreds of sub-postmasters across the UK were wrongly convicted for stealing money – from their own branches – by the company that trusted them to serve their communities. A story that was described by a leading barrister in a landmark High Court hearing in 2019 as "the biggest miscarriage of justice in UK legal history". It's a tale of corporate malfeasance involving a wholly state-owned company, an institution set up way back in 1660, which actually precedes the actual creation of the UK state itself in 1707.

Also intimately involved in the story are a multinational billion-pound IT company – Fujitsu from Japan – and three Westminster governments, which saw each one of the UK's main political parties – Labour, Conservative and the Liberal Democrats – equally culpable in what transpired.

Despite its twenty-year plus history, it's also an ongoing story in view of the statutory public inquiry under the chairmanship of Welshman Sir Wyn Williams, which has now been in session since June 2021.

There is still no sign of all the issues being successfully resolved for the wronged sub-postmasters, despite winning two court cases over the past four years. And tragically, no less than sixty-one of those sub-postmasters have died before receiving due compensation.

The scale of what's actually gone on is almost impossible to take in on so many levels. But a story on such a macro level often needs to be explained on a micro level to be fully understood and fully appreciated.

The Stamp of Innocence will seek to tell this shocking story through the eyes of one ordinary Welsh sub-postmaster and his family, who were caught up in this nightmare for sixteen long years. It's a tale about one man, Hughie Noel Thomas. A man broken on the wheel of an unfeeling and broken system. An innocent man, jailed for a crime he simply did not commit. A man tortured by the loss of his good name and reputation built up locally for over half a century, and haunted for years and years by what was done to him by a wholly state-owned company.

But it's also a redemptive tale about one man's epic fight to clear his name and restore his honour. Noel Thomas can be seen almost like a David-like figure taking on the Goliath of the Post Office with all its power, prestige and influence – underpinned, of course, by having His Majesty's Government as its sole shareholder.

The story will also be told through a special father-and-daughter prism as Sian Thomas, Noel's daughter, developed a key role for herself as her father's fiercest defender over the years. She was the family's advocate throughout the saga, devoting years of her life to researching what happened to her father, learning about the justice system and networking as she went along.

It's a story about a family. But it's a story about a community, too. A story about an island – Ynys Môn (Anglesey) in Wales – where family, belonging, spirituality, language and roots are still paramount. These are, perhaps, even essential as an island on the periphery, so far from the centres of power, money and influence, both in a Welsh context and a UK context. A world apart, you could say, from the soulless, corporate, technological world that is so dominant in our modern society today.

In the 1950s, the Christian author CS Lewis warned that a day was fast approaching when technology would be placed above man himself. Technology, he said, would be worshipped and idolised and considered more important and dependable than mere humankind.

The Stamp of Innocence will show how CS Lewis's prediction came so horribly true in Noel Thomas's life and in so many other sub-postmasters' lives as well. His words being not only a fulfilled prophecy for our times, but a warning for the future as well, in view of an increasing technocratic agenda being imposed on society by governments and corporations.

This is a tale that invites us to take stock and to consider whether we want technology to have so much control over us in the future, when it can go so horribly wrong – as seen in the Post Office scandal.

* * *

I would like to thank Noel Thomas for devoting so much of his time to sharing his experiences with me for this book. Noel did this in a very open and honest way at all times, even though bringing all those memories to mind again often proved to be a difficult and painful experience for him.

I'm also very thankful to Sian Thomas for her help in preparing this book. All her dogged research work, along with all the valuable connections she has developed over the past few years, served to make my task that much easier.

I feel incredibly privileged to have helped Noel and Sian get their incredible story out to the wider public. Their sincere wish is that sharing their story might help ensure that something like this can never happen again.

I also want to thank all the individuals who enabled this book to be written by supporting a Crowdfunder appeal launched by Sian Thomas. Over £9,000 was raised in just two months. The names of all those who contributed towards this appeal will appear at the end of the book.

Finally, I'd like to thank the team at Troubador Publishing for all their help and support in producing this book. Their professionalism has enabled this project to be turned around much quicker than I had anticipated.

Thank you to all concerned.

ALED GWYN JÔB
September 2023

CHAPTER 1

The First Night Inside

Noel

BANG!

A big, black door closes on the very worst day of my whole life.

I find myself in a small, dark, slovenly cell.

This place is.

Walton.

Prison.

Two bunks, four walls, a narrow window.

I swallow. And swallow again.

And then the noise starts up…

The shouting. The yelling. The screaming.

The non-stop banging on the doors.

Other people. People like me. Who have landed in here.

From somewhere, the words of that old Welsh hymn came to mind: *Pan oeddem ni mewn carchar tywyll du…* ('When we were once in a dark, dark prison…').

Sung it so many times over the years.

Never to think or imagine this would ever come true.

And happen in my own life. Here. Now.

I lie down in complete exhaustion on the bottom bunk in my own clothes.

No pyjamas, no overnight bag, nothing at all.

Only a hard mattress and a thin blanket. And a broken heart.

And the noise… the noise…

Then starting up in my own head.

Just as noisy and just as non-stop.

Going round and round and round.

How on earth can someone go from *paradwys* ('paradise'), that safe and warm place where I was brought up, and then land up in this dangerous hell.

And talking of hell – why the hell did I listen to Wyn Jones and plead guilty in that court? He promised me that pleading guilty in court would keep me out of jail. He promised me!

Yet here I am, for all those words of his.

And why didn't that blooming call centre listen to me?

How many times did I phone them to say there were problems with the Horizon system – ten, twelve times for sure…

Warm words again: "Don't worry… everything will be okay."

Words that betrayed me… Words that let me down… Words that…

"So, what are you in for, mate?"

A strong Scouse voice.

From the upper bunk, cutting across my dark thoughts.

And then having to tell him that I had been jailed for stealing from the Post Office.

Wrongly imprisoned.

"Yeah, sure, mate. We've all got to say that, haven't we, to keep ourselves going in here."

The cynical tone like a sledgehammer to the head.

Was this a dose of reality from the Scouser? Was I just imagining things?

Had I actually missed something in my constant revisiting of the past?

But Ian's chat was still comforting in a way.

Keeping me going for a while.

Hearing him talk about his experiences in and out of jails all through his life.

A proud jailbird, in a way.

A bit of a moiderer, maybe, but yet, so good to be able to switch off for a while.

From all those deep and dark paths I was going down in my own mind.

But then absolute silence, as he fell asleep.

And then I plunged back into the darkness… into my own disturbing thoughts.

Not able to sleep, not able to settle, not able to believe all this.

So many thoughts, so many fears, so many worries churning around in my mind.

This place was so… terrifying.

I felt like Daniel thrown into a modern lion's den.

And who knew what kind of lions would be waiting in here to devour me?

2am… 3am… 4am… 5am…

With the clock on the wall moving forwards in a snail-like fashion. Agonisingly slowly.

And this snail of a clock as if it was gaining some pleasure watching me watching it.

How did that hymn go again? Oh yes… *Goleuni* ('Light')… *Rhoist in oleuni nefol* ('You gave us heavenly light').

Huh! Any light seems very far away in here, I can tell you!

In this pit. In this hell… In this…

Heavens above… what would poor Mam and Dad make of all this?

I break into an instant cold sweat just thinking about it.

Thank God they've gone from this crazy, messed-up world we live in right now.

But the rest of the family are still here. Still in the epicentre of the storm.

How on earth are they going to cope with all this?

They're the ones who will have to face the music – and face the public after all the media storm.

With me stuck inside. For how long? Nine months?

"Nine months. Take him down…"

Remembering the hard and cold words of the judge that morning was like receiving another sledgehammer blow.

Another flash – the faces of Eira, Sian, Edwin, Arfon and Auntie Gwenda in the public gallery and their ashen, shocked faces looking down on me in the dock.

What's going to happen to them?

What's going to happen to the post in Gaerwen now that they've closed it?

What's going to happen to the customers?

Questions. Questions. One after the other.

Clock saying 5am now.

The shouting and screaming starts up all round me again.

Maybe that's what I should do as well.

I want to shout and scream as well.

Not just lie down, limply… helplessly, like this.

But then, I'm not like that.

That fight is not in me.

Sian, my daughter, is the fighter in our family – not me…

Zzzzzzzzzzzzzzzzzzzzzzzzzz. Zzzzzzzzzzzzzzzzzzzzzzzzzz.

Ian's snoring from the top bunk cuts across my thoughts again.

He's obviously settled in well in here.

Settled in again. Sleep coming so easily for him.

Finally, some form of sleep comes my way.

And I can escape.

Now, I'm riding my bike again.

Down through Paradwys, down that old hill again.

It's early morning and I'm on my first round again as a postman.

The mountains ahead of me. The years ahead of me. The wind through my hair and I'm feeling so free, so free…

"Let's be having you!" A crass voice interrupts my dream and drags me off the bike. From paradise back to hell.

I struggle to open my tired eyes. To see a figure, clad all in black, right in front of me.

One of the jail officers in his uniform standing in front of the bunks.

It's half past six and breakfast will be served in an hour.

But I don't want any food. I just want to return to my dream. Back on the bike.

Noel on the bike. As it used to be. Before this shitshow.

"C'mon, mate. You've just got to make the best of it now. The sooner you accept that, the easier it gets in here."

Ian's voice from the top bunk.

I want to scream at him that I'm innocent. That I haven't done anything. That my family need me.

But what's the point?

He looks as if he's someone who's heard all this before. From many fellow jailbirds over the years. And is heartily fed-up of hearing it as well.

There's nothing for it but to drag myself somehow from the bunk and make my way groggily to the toilet at the far end of the cell.

A memory flashes across my mind: *The Waltons*.

I used to like that series on TV years ago.

"Night, John Boy." "Night, Mary Ellen." "Night, Erin." "Night, Grandma." "Night, Grand-Pa."

That warm exchange of goodnight greetings. The closeness of that bond. The warmth I had at home with my own family.

But thinking about the Waltons is a stake through the heart.

No family. No warmth. No comfort. No light. No love.

I break down in tears in the pokey toilet at the end of the cell. How on earth has it come to this for me? How have I managed to find myself in such a hellish situation as this?

"C'mon, soft lad." The Scouser knocking at the door this time. Knocking again.

I can't move for a while. As if I'm frozen solid on the toilet seat. But out I come, with the tears still pouring down my cheeks. To face the hell ahead of me.

CHAPTER 2

A Precious Place to Call My Home

"On a small island, the past is vastly alive and the future is not separated."

DH Lawrence

There's no fewer than 6,289 small islands on the archipelago of the UK and islands are deeply woven into our collective memories as people on these isles.

A small island can be seen as a metaphor for a person's life, suggests author Patrick Barkham, and the role of Ynys Môn (Anglesey) does indeed play a leading role in *The Stamp of Innocence*. In this story about a proud islander, Noel Thomas's relationship with his island colours every aspect of the tale in some shape or form.

Ynys Môn (population 70,000) is a small island at the top of Wales, which literally looks like the head on the body of Wales as a nation – a fact much to the delight of its inhabitants, who have a very distinct island identity and a sense of themselves as being set apart from their fellow countrymen.

Even a cut above, you could say.

And, indeed, we as islanders have history on our side with all of this.

The island is fondly referred to as Mon Mam Cymru ('Mon the Mother of Wales'). It is a reference to centuries past, when the island was known as the granary of Wales because of its bread-producing capacity for the whole of the nation.

In the complex and convoluted history between Wales and England, it's no coincidence that one of the main tactics used by a succession of English kings in seeking to subdue Wales was to target Ynys Môn, mainly by sea, so as to cut off food supplies to the rest of Wales and throttle any disobedience – which tended to happen quite a lot over the centuries.

This 'target the head' strategy also chimes with another very important chapter during the island's more distant history as well. Ynys Môn was revered at one time as the sanctuary of the druids – the spiritual and political leaders of the old Brittanic tribes, so feared by the Romans, who conquered Britain in the 1st Century. The druids ('Y Derwyddon' in Welsh) were known as the spiritual, moral and educational leaders of the tribes who lived in Wales and other parts of the UK before the Roman Conquest. With Ynys Môn recognised as their main fortress, the training of a druid could take up to twenty years in all.

The druids did not keep any written records and all their learning was based on an oral tradition passed on over the generations. This was due to their very pragmatic belief that life was ever-changing and shifting and that writing their beliefs down at any one point could actually turn them into stiff and inflexible dogma not capable of meeting the new challenges of life.

They also believed that retaining all information orally was an excellent way to develop thinking skills and memory, and to ensure that it would be more difficult for their culture to be destroyed.

Their underlying belief structure was to be *dewr a daionus* ('brave and virtuous') – qualities that have stood the test of time in Wales, as this modern-day story will attest.

Such was their influence over the tribes of Ancient Britain, the invading Romans decided the druids had to be wiped out completely in order to demoralise the native Britons. A 'target the head' strategy was finally enacted in the year 57 BC according to Roman sources.

It all makes for thrilling reading with the first Roman sortie scared away by the appearance of hundreds of Druidic women, all dressed in black on the shores of the island, shrieking profane curses at the Romans. The poor Romans took fright hearing the ladies of the island performing in such a manner and decided to call off the whole invasion. Unfortunately, the Romans were stiffened up by their generals and returned to the island a few years later, where they massacred the druids, desecrating all their secret groves and shrines on the island.

They say that the past is unusually present on small islands – and of a summer evening here, as the sun goes down and the darkness creeps over the land, you can almost sense that ancient druidic heritage still calling out to you despite all the centuries that have elapsed. You intuit as well that the old pagan influences – the reverence for land and sky and sea – are still very much to the fore right across the island, with a resurgence to be seen in our modern times.

The 2021 census in Wales shows that an increasing number here are now describing themselves as Pagan. And with a number of pre-historic sites such as Barclodiad y Gawres, and Bryn Celli Ddu dotted around Ynys Môn, there's no getting away from all these influences.

But then Ynys Môn also has 1,500 years of Christian heritage, which has shaped and moulded the island and its people for time immemorial. No less than fifty-three villages here start with *Llan* ('church'), giving an indication of how many settlements actually developed with the planting of a church here. And some villages are lucky enough to have had two saints in place, such as Llanddeusant (the settlement of two saints) and nearby

Llantrisant (the settlement of three saints), which goes to show the impact that Celtic Christianity has had on the island over many centuries.

Some of the early Christian saints who settled here, such as Cybi and Seiriol, have been immortalised by the old story that the two saints would walk to meet each other each day in the centre of the island. With one of them facing the sun, *Cybi Felyn* ('Yellow Cybi'), and *Seiriol Wyn* (White Seiriol) facing away from the sun on their respective journeys.

It's this vibrant Pagan-Christian heritage that makes Ynys Môn such an intriguing place. The deep connection to the past and its two traditions have shaped and created this island across the centuries.

All of which has been mediated, of course, throughout its long history through the medium of the national language, *Cymraeg* ('Welsh'). Even today, with all the pressures of the modern world impinging on the island, it remains the second most Welsh-speaking county in the whole of Wales, with not far short of sixty per cent of the population able to speak the language. The rootedness and richness of this language is what really waters the soil of this island day in, day out.

In an age where technology and technocracy are becoming ever more oppressive in people's lives (as will be shown graphically in this book), there's a primal spirit to be felt on Ynys Môn. A connection to land, culture, language, history and natural beauty, which stands as a welcome counterpoint to all the disturbing manifestations of modernity. Along with a growing sense of how modernity is fast ruining this precious heritage.

As this book is going to print, a campaign is in place to save Penrhos – a nature reserve on Ynys Cybi, an island within an island, which is to be sacrificed so that developers can build holiday chalets on the land. The ancient woodland is to be moved to another part of Holyhead that has been used for years as a waste ground. A company called 'Land and Lakes' want to develop the holiday chalets, with the local council, seemingly bound by previous planning permission granted for the scheme, unable to do anything but approve it. Protestors are now planning court action to save Penrhos with a crowdfunding appeal in motion to pay for this action. There is a sense that something sacred is being sacrificed here to appease the Mammon of our age.

The tourist industry is a lifeline for many on the island, especially in view of the lack of general employment opportunities. But there is a real danger of killing the golden goose with the current overdevelopment.

One of the abiding memories people have here of the Covid period was the quietness and tranquillity during the early months of 2020, when people believed that Covid 19 was much worse than it actually turned out to be.

A time when mass public travel for leisure and tourism came to an end for months at a time. Many still remember those warm months with fondness, as if the island had been returned to its own inhabitants. It was as if it became a precious home again – and the island thrown back to earlier times of less bustle, less hurry, less traffic, less stress and less tension for all. As if we had gone back to the 1950s in a sense.

This sentiment provides an essential background for this book, the story of Noel Thomas and his long personal ordeal at the hands of the Post Office. As you can only properly understand Noel's story through understanding his own relationship with Ynys Môn and its people. And how that interplay between land and people has coloured everything about his outlook on life.

As an islander through and through, you have to appreciate what happened to him through the eyes of an islander. His wide network of family and community relationships on the island shine a bright light on the island mentality in general, which involves a unique way of looking at life all round.

It's an island very far from the corridors of power and influence in Westminster and London, and increasingly shut out of a new

Welsh order, too, with Cardiff being so dominant in Welsh life, while rural areas such as Ynys Môn are often considered to be irrelevant and on the periphery by politicians of all colours.

The *Monwysion* ('Islanders') thus always have to fall back on their own resources – their language, their family and community networks, their land, their spirituality – and live life on their own terms in a way that stays true to their own traditions.

We'll now let Noel introduce you to his home, his identity, his island, his muse in his own words.

***

Noel

I was born a day before Christmas in 1946 and my present for that was to be named Noel! It seems it was a local canon, Canon Orig Evans from Trefdraeth, who suggested the name to my father, which shows that the church has always played a big part in my life from the very start in a way.

I must have been a bit of a surprise because my parents were late getting married and nobody came along after me either. Maybe surprises are part and parcel of the family since the story is that the Thomases started on Ynys Môn after a young girl, who was pregnant, was rowed to the island from another island (Bardsey) just before the child was born.

Apparently, the child – my great grandfather – was the illegitimate son of Thomas Williams, who had taken upon himself the title of 'The King of Enlli', along with his own throne and crown to match his title! Jane Thomas, the mother, who was born in 1789, therefore moved from one island to another island and obviously settled very well here, having a further fourteen children!

It's odd in a way, but I've always felt a pull towards Ynys Enlli and I've always said I'd like to go there one day. An islander drawn to another island. The idea of being related to a 'king' is also quite ironic in view of the fact that the Royal Mail came to play such an important part of my life in several ways, and change my life beyond recognition.

When I was three, we moved a few miles from Trefdraeth to live in Malltraeth as my mother, Annie Mary, took over the Bodfal House business from her mother, Kate Jones, who had run the business for a number of years. Bodfal House was a traditional village shop, the kind we used to have years ago, selling everything you could possibly want. It came to play a very important part in my life. My Nain (grandmother), Kate Jones, also lived with us in Bodfal House and she was a huge influence on me as I was growing up. She was the chief, for sure!

What I remember from the very start was being brought up in the business and being a key part of it in many ways. I was told from the outset that if I wanted any pocket money, I had to help out in the business and the home as well. I think I was around six years old when I started to help out for real in the shop, placing items on the counters and serving behind the counter.

I can well remember putting my mam in a tight spot once. A customer came into the shop, asking for something or other, and Mam told her: "We don't have that I'm very sorry…"

And I piped up, "But Mam. We've got some of that under the counter here!"

I had a piece of her mind after that, you can be sure.

Mam was the scholar when it came to running the business, even though my father, Hugh – who used to be a signalman on the railway – also helped with the day-to-day running of Bodfal House. She was brilliant with people, always making time for her customers and always ready to listen to their stories and problems, whatever they might be. My father often became very irate at all this non-stop chatting in the shop and I remember him saying to her once: "Annie Mary, you have taken over half an hour to sell anything to that customer. All you do with them is chat!"

But my mother was very discerning in her way and how she listened to people's stories. She would have one story from this customer and a counter-story from another customer and then she had to balance them in her mind and try to work out what the real story was! As she was so good at listening, she also had skills as a kind of counsellor in a way, I think, and certainly seeing her doing that so easily for so many years was an education in itself for me. Who knows, maybe I became a councillor later down the line after the counselling I saw my mam delivering for so long.

My father, Hugh, was a very different character to my mam, being more sharpish in many ways, with precious little time for all the niceties that had to go on in a village shop. He certainly didn't have my mam's diplomatic skills, for sure, often being frustrated at having to deal with different, sometimes difficult, customers and pander to their needs all the time. I remember him complaining about this to my mam one night over supper and her responding, "Hugh, you've got to learn to kiss ass without getting your lips dirty!"

But he was a very busy individual in his own right, helping out with two businesses (Bodfal House and Siop Newydd, which we bought later on), while also being a keen gardener and a successful competitor in flower competitions. He was also responsible for looking after the pigs we had at the back of Bodfal House, which also came in very handy for the family business in various ways.

However, my father came a cropper with the pigs one day, as he managed to incur the wrath of the chief (my grandmother). He came across a famous island character called Johnnie Moch (Johnny Pigs) who managed to persuade him to sell the pigs to him one Christmas. However, the physical transaction happened early on a Sunday morning and who heard it all from their bedroom? My grandmother! She kept it under a hat for a few days and then summoned my father to her room for a dressing-down. Not only was it a crime to have done this on a Sunday, but somehow she had managed to find out that my father had been short-changed by Johnny Moch as well! Which was almost as bad a sin as the first in her eyes! I can still remember my father walking across the landing from her room, saying, under his breath, "How the hell did she find about all that?"

Business was in the blood in our family as Uncle Bob, Mam's brother, kept the Joiners Arms, right next to Bodfal House, and I spent a lot of time in Uncle Bob and Auntie Nellie's company. I spent just as much time in that business as the shop to all intents and purposes. And with Uncle Bob and Auntie Nellie being childless, it was almost as if I was brought up with two fathers and two mothers in effect. How lucky was I!

The time spent at the Joiners gave me an opportunity to spend some time with another section of the community who were older than me, learning to enjoy their company as well. More often than not, I would be curled up on the sofa with Auntie Nellie in the lounge of the Joiners on a Saturday night watching television – and hearing everything that went on in the pub at the same time! I'll never forget one funny incident at the Joiners one Saturday evening, when I was slightly older and helping Uncle Bob behind the bar.

A couple used to come in every Saturday night and the lady always came in with her little poodle, who used to accompany her everywhere. Anyway, the couple were sitting down with their drink next to Huw Glo, who was quite a local character for sure. The little poodle was on the lady's lap as usual, with its behind pointing at Huw. For a laugh, he put his cigarette into its behind. Well, it gave out a huge yelp and jumped a few feet in the air.

"*Duwcs*, what's up with little poodle tonight?" asked Huw, innocently.

Well, the lady rushed out of the pub with the poodle in her arms and her poor husband had to follow her home without having more than a sip of his pint that night!

What I remember so fondly about this time of growing up in the village was the leg-pulling and the light-heartedness between people. And everyone being totally comfortable with all that. Certainly there was none of this taking perpetual offence about everything that we see in today's society! Everyone seemed to be more tolerant of each other somehow and willing to give everyone the benefit of the doubt on things. After all, weren't we all just part of one community, after all?

Growing up in Malltraeth in the 1950s and 1960s was a very enjoyable, if not perfect, experience for a young lad. The post-war rations had come to an end in 1952 and life was gradually starting to improve for all of us and everything seemed to be on the up. There was a safe and warm feeling associated with living in Malltraeth at that time, with around two hundred people living there. I knew every single soul. Every single one – young, middle-aged and old. All of us were like one big family somehow.

What I remember very fondly was the ability to wander around the area so easily, with no limitations in place at all. I could be out for hours and hours in summer as nobody was at all worried about us. This wandering as children was totally natural and we all felt totally safe. Our parents felt just as safe with this arrangement.

I could easily call at people's houses at any time and know that there would be a warm welcome for me at all times. Sometimes, I went to watch television with Jim Fidler, who lived across the way to us. At the start of the 1950s, only three houses had televisions and Jim Fidler was one of those. It was seen as a luxury and I felt that I was having one huge treat in being able to go and watch television with Uncle Jim. He came from Wrecsam originally and had a cigarette clamped in his mouth day in, day out. It was in Jim's house that I had one of the formative experiences in my life as a child, because it was in Jim's house that I saw a naked woman for the first time!

I was in the lounge one evening watching TV as usual and the next thing I knew Mrs Fidler walked in with no clothes on at all, for some reason! I'll never forget Jim shouting at her at the top of his voice, "For God's sake, woman, put some clothes on!" and me just standing there not knowing where to look or what to say!

Malltraeth at that time was a community-orientated place and it had plenty going on there. It was also a big help, of course, that everyone was employed, as part of the effort to put the country back on its feet after the war. People in the village worked on the railway, at Niwbwrch Forest, Ty Croes camp, on farms, at the Creamery in Llangefni and there were no less than five shops in the village: Bodfal House, Siop Newydd, Siop Pritchard, a small Post Office and Ensor Butchers.

Everybody seemed to be so happy after the war, anticipating that life could only get better, and this sentiment or feeling was shared by one and all. There certainly wasn't this huge sense of isolation that people complain about today and I'd venture to say, as well, that there was much less of this depression and anxiety that seems so widespread in today's society among people of all ages.

It breaks my heart to see Malltraeth, my home village today, to be honest, as it's changed so much. With no fewer than twenty-one houses on the high street being second homes. Even Sardis Chapel – one of the oldest buildings in the village – has been sold recently for £1.4 million, which, of course, is way above the price that any local person could afford! The housing market has become an oppressive force on local people, with one recent study showing that Ynys Môn had seen the sharpest increase in second homes in Wales over the past ten years.

Unfortunately, this has contributed to the anglicisation of the island and a shocking decline in the fortunes of Welsh almost under our noses over the past generation or so. I think our politicians, both locally and nationally, have to get to grips with this situation. Otherwise, Welsh will stop being a living community language here. And all the Welsh signs in the world won't bring that back!

We've all heard of Areas of Natural Beauty. Well, personally, I believe Ynys Môn should be declared an Area of Natural Language – with the language given exactly the same status and protection that our landscapes have. Perhaps we need to introduce some licensing system where people who move here to live should be expected to learn Welsh, say, within two years of their move. Yes, some serious resources would need to be ploughed into all this, but if we are serious about our language and ensuring a future for it, it really is time to do this.

Surely, we can't stand back and watch a language that has been spoken here for 1,500 years disappear without doing something about that? '*O bydded i'r hen iaith barhau*', as the last line of the national anthem goes ('Let's ensure the old language persists').

Although I am now a churchgoer, I was brought up chapel, which was another important influence as I was growing up. We used to attend services every Sunday in the Weslean Cause at the top of the village. More often than not, the minister came to us for Sunday lunch afterwards, so I had to be on best behaviour!

Like in the rest of the village, there were some real characters in the chapel, such as Miss Thomas Pen Parc. She had this huge hymn book she carried with her everywhere, but could not sing a note. She also gave me a telling off one time in a '*cymanfa ganu*' ('singing festival') for sitting in her seat. She had paid for that seat, thank you very much! She was quite eccentric and had a pet cow, who dressed in quite a fancy coat for some reason.

I remember being in the Joiners one evening when Roger, who was responsible for fallen stock in the area, came in and asked where Miss Thomas lived, since he needed to collect a fallen animal from her property. As I knew her, I volunteered to take Roger there. And once I got there, I was press-ganged into holding the horns of this cow while he delivered the fatal shot to her.

"Go and ask Miss Thomas if she wants to keep the coat that this stupid cow is wearing," he told me.

"Of course I do!" she replied to me indignantly at the door, as if I had just asked the most ridiculous and insulting question ever!

For me, it really was like living in paradise growing up in Malltraeth in the 1950s and 1960s. Quite literally so, since part of the area was called Paradwys – the Welsh word for 'paradise'! Paradwys was also where I got my first job as a postman after leaving school, although I had a brief stint at the marine yard in Holyhead before that. Looking back now, it seems almost incredible that I could do a round of seventeen miles every morning on a bike, but I was young, fit and carefree, so I thought nothing of it!

I had, by then, discovered another form of paradise, as I had met Eira, who as to become my wife and the mother of my three children. I first saw Eira through the window of the John Edwards store in Menai Bridge where she worked – talk about window-shopping! I then met up with her on a night out in Bangor and the rest, as they say, is history.

But exactly at the same time as my personal paradise was opening up, it seemed that the paradise enjoyed by small villages stores like Bodfal House for so long was coming to an end. You see, in 1974, the first Kwik Supermarket opened up in Llanfairpwll – the first supermarket to open on Ynys Môn, and the start of their huge dominance over our food and our whole lives. Small village stores just could not compete with the choice and the competitiveness of these supermarkets.

It was a big blow to my parents, who had run their two village stores so effectively and so loyally for so many years, but a new tide was coming in and there was no turning it back unfortunately.

I think my mother had sensed that the writing was on the wall two years previous to this with the introduction of decimalisation in 1972 – '*y pres gwirion*' ('the funny money'), as she termed it. She decided to pass on the business to myself and Eira at that point. It was the start of the end for the other small shops in the village as well, and it is such a shame to see the village today being a shell of what it used to be years ago, with all its liveliness, vibrancy and hope for the future.

Looking back at those early years, there's no doubt in my mind that the business experiences I had in Bodfal House, Siop Newydd and in the Joiners proved to be a huge influence over my future direction in life. It was such a wonderful introduction to speaking to people, listening to people, dealing with people and understanding people. These skills would serve me well in the roles that came my way in the years to come, as a postman, a postmaster and a councillor.

A skill that has stayed with me all these years is the skill of knowing when to say something and when to hold back. And for that I thank my mother, father, Uncle Bob, Auntie Nellie and everybody else who made my upbringing such a sociable experience in that little village – Malltraeth – which is still so close to my heart.

CHAPTER 3

Deepening the Connection

Noel

One of the privileges that came my way during my working life was to deepen my connection with this wonderful island of mine: Mon Mam Cymru. As a postman, working the rounds for twenty years, I was able to deepen my connection with what is known as the inner island and the outer island. The inner island being the communities of Malltraeth, Llangefni, Rhosmeirch, Capel Coch and Pentraeth, which are still, to this day, predominantly Welsh-speaking areas. The outer island comprises the communities of Rhosneigr and Benllech – on opposite sides of the island – which are now more English-speaking in nature, mainly because of the effects of the tourism industry on the island for many years. Luckily, for me, being such a people person and so sociable after my upbringing in Malltraeth, I was just as home in the two scenarios.

I always counted my blessings in being able to get to know new areas on the island and new people, too – and, indeed, to be able to make friends with many of them as well. Nowadays, as we know, our poor postmen are monitored and tracked endlessly by the Post Office. They can't even sneeze without the Post Office knowing about it! In my day, there was no such intrusive tracking at all. As long as you completed your round and did your job properly, there were no questions asked. This meant that there was always time to chat with your customers, to get to know them and build a real connection with them, which was so valuable.

And there was time, as well, to come across so many characters in different areas, who really livened up your day and made your job so very interesting and stimulating in many ways. One such character was the well-known doctor, Dr John Hughes of Llangefni. He was a legendary figure in the Llangefni area for many years, who everybody knew and who had a great sense of humour as well.

I'll never forget going to deliver a parcel for an old lady once in Capel Coch and sitting there having a *panad* (a 'cuppa') as she waited for Dr Hughes to come and see her for a chest complaint she had.

I was in the kitchen having my cuppa and she was in bed in the room next door, wrapped in several layers of shawls to keep warm.

Dr Hughes came in and said to me, "What are you doing here again?"

"Postman!" I replied.

"Huh! Don't you get everywhere," he snorted in that nasal drawl of his.

Then he went next door into the bedroom to inspect her chest, exclaiming loudly, "Salome and the Seven Veils!" on seeing Mrs Williams with all the different layers she had to take off for Dr Hughes to do his work.

That was Dr Hughes for you; you could always rely on him to see the funny side of things in any situation and be able to cheer people up whatever the circumstances were. They do say, 'Laughter is the best medicine', don't they? (Sidenote from ghostwriter: I remember going to see Dr Hughes once as a teenager, having hurt my foot. Dr. Hughes's response: "You poor lad, one of your father's heavy sermons has fallen on your foot again, I see!")

One of the things I had to do during my spell as a postman was to attend various courses and the like. I'll never forget travelling down to Cardiff for one course, with a very old-fashioned guy called Wil Tan coming along with us as well. Poor old Wil had never been so far away from home before and he had to phone his wife three times a day to assure her that he was okay.

Anyway, one night, we went for a pint in one of the pubs in Bute Town, Cardiff Bay – when it was very different to what it is today. We met up with some real characters from the north-east, who soon cottoned on to the fact that Wil was a bit naïve, if you like.

One of them said to me at the bar, "Let's have a bit of fun with old Wil."

He then introduced us to a couple of ladies of the night who were sitting opposite us at the bar and we sat down with them at a table nearby.

Well, one of these ladies of the night forced Wil to sit on her lap and started to play with his hair, asking him, repeatedly, "Tell me your name, darling? What's your name, sweetheart?"

I've never, ever in my life, seen anybody sweat as much as Wil did at the table that night. The sweat was pouring out of him from every crevice in his body it seemed to me. Poor old Wil was squirming in his seat, not knowing how to handle this bold lady of the night.

Well, she then got up at one point. And Wil jumped up and bolted out of the pub – and ran all the way back to the hotel such was his panic at having been put in such an uncompromising situation! All he said to me the next morning was: "Just you make sure that hers indoors never hears about what went on last night!"

Another interesting incident that I came across during my duties as a postman was a huge drug-smuggling event, which became a major talking point locally and further afield. The cache was smuggled in to Ynys Llanddwyn (a well-known local beauty spot named after another saint, Santes Dwynwen – the patron saint of Welsh lovers) and then hidden away in some big bails on a local farm, Ty'n Llwyn, in Paradwys. The incident gained huge media attention and eventually resulted in three men being charged and imprisoned for drug smuggling.

Funnily enough, I got to know about the whole story in much more details a couple of years down the line, when I went down for a few days to visit my cousin in the valleys. When we went out for a pint one night, I saw a familiar face standing at the bar. I was racking my brains, thinking: *Where have I seen this guy before?*

Anyway, after having a few sips of my pint, I went up to him and asked him: "Don't I know you from somewhere?"

"You should," he replied, instantly. "We used to play darts together in that pub at Malltraeth!"

He was an undercover agent who had been working on the drug-smuggling case for some three months or so. When I played darts with him in the Joiners Arms, his story was that he was working at Rio Tinto – a big aluminium-producing company at Holyhead on a short-term project. But the truth of the matter was that has spending hours and hours at night stalking out the forest at Niwbwrch (New Borough), attempting to collect evidence on those who were involved with the drug smuggling. He proceeded to tell me a good deal more about the whole saga over a pint or two at Ynys Hir that evening!

One of the things I learnt from my parents and the wider community where I grew up was not just a liking for people, but also a sense of *chwarae teg* ('fair play') and a willingness to speak out if I came across any unfairness in life.

In the 1980s, when the old Post Office shut in Llangefni, we, as local postmen, had been placed in a portacabin on the industrial estate in Llangefni. By this time, the post in Llangefni had expanded quite significantly as a number of smaller Post Offices had been closed on the island, with the operation being centralised at Llangefni. This was only supposed to be a short-term arrangement as the Portakabins were really unsuitable for us as workers and everybody was complaining about things as the months wore on, with no sign of a new office space being introduced.

I decided to speak up on behalf of all of us, as the Post Office had specifically promised us a new office in closing the old centre, and I sent a letter to the Post Office in Chester, outlining our case. The Post then sent a huge six foot four guy over to Llangefni to discuss things with the workers. When I walked into the office, he was sitting with his feet on the table and bellowed at me: "I want to talk to you!"

"I want to talk to you as well," I replied. "When you take your feet off the desk, I will talk with you," and turned away to leave the office.

He jumped up and rushed to the door. "Come back! Come here – you're getting a new office!"

And in 1991, after all the wait we had to endure, a new office eventually arrived for us, showing yet again that sometimes you have to speak up and speak out in life to make a difference. I've always tried to do that, I think.

One understanding that came my way as a postman on the island was to discover the hold that large landowners still have here on society, even in the 21st century.

From what I understand, many of these landed families on Ynys Môn received their large portions of land here for supporting the right side in the Civil War, which took place between the Royalists and Parliamentarians back in the 1640s! Their influence can be seen today, such as the Meyricks of Bodorgan, who still hold swathes of land on the island, along with the influence and clout that affords them. It really makes a mockery of the idea that we are living in a modern democracy when these landed gentry can still hold so much power in our lives.

Anyway, we, as postmen, were not allowed to go down the road to Plas Bodorgan – the Meyrick's palace – as it was out of bounds for some reason. One time, I ventured to drive the van all the way to Plas Bodorgan and, within minutes, the estate's agent had phoned the office in Bangor to complain about me!

I was then called in to see Mr Thomas the Postmaster to get the third-degree treatment for such an appalling offence. Mr Thomas went through the motions with all this, before asking me innocently at the end: "By the way, Noel, do you want to buy a raffle ticket?" He was very involved with the football club in Beaumaris and was obviously thinking about the welfare of the football club even when giving me a row! This little incident showed the human side of life working at the Post Office, which I appreciated so much – before technology and this obsessive managerial culture took over.

One of the unofficial jobs of the postman at this time was carrying news from village to village. After all, there were only three television channels at the time and no social media, and no real way for people to share information with each other as happens so easily today.

It was amazing how I was quizzed relentlessly by people about what was happening in such-and-such a place! People were seemingly of the opinion that the postman was a fount of information about everything that was going on. Well, I've always had a good ear and a good memory as well, so I always did my best to keep people in the loop, so to speak!

After moving to become a sub-postmaster in Gaerwen, I was then able to deepen my connection again with the island after I was elected a councillor on the local authority, Cyngor Ynys Môn/Anglesey County Council. This allowed me to meet other councillors from other parts of the island and to take part in decisions affecting the whole island.

As it happens, before I went for it, I asked the opinion of a seasoned councillor, who had known me since I was a small boy, Mrs ME Edward – one of the few females on the council at the time, but a very influential one as well. I remember sitting in her kitchen as if it was yesterday, having a cup of tea and telling her I was thinking of putting myself up for the vacant seat in Gaerwen. She looked at me and said, "Well, Noel, we've got enough silly buggers in the council as it is, so we might as well have another one in the ranks!" I think you could call that a back-handed compliment!

Anyway, I went for it as an independent candidate, standing

against another independent candidate, Raymond Evans. Raymond was the favourite as he had been living in the area much longer than I had. However, when the result came through, I had managed to get 468 votes against Raymond's 325. I was a local councillor! It was an amazing feeling to think that the people of Gaerwen had put their trust in me and were now depending on me to speak on their behalf in the county council. It was quite a humbling experience, to be honest, but I knew, full well, that there was a hard task ahead of me to understand how the council operated and what exactly what was expected from a local councillor etc.

Even so, I did not imagine for a minute how much of an education was awaiting me on the council – in more than one way! You see, by 1992, Ynys Môn Council had come to the attention of the whole of Wales and not for good reasons, unfortunately. There were a range of problems including dodgy planning decisions, individuals accused of abusing their power and general concerns about the behaviour of individual councillors and how the council itself was being run.

Indeed, there were several television programmes about it and the local press had enough stories to keep them busy for years as a result! It really was a crying shame because all this negative publicity about the council seemed to paint all of us with the same brush –other parts of Wales seemed to relish calling us 'the corruption capital of Cymru'! It really wasn't a good time to tell other people you came from Ynys Môn, because you knew that the automatic response would be: "Oh yes, we've heard all about what goes on up there!" You would laugh it off at the time, of course, but it still hurt that people had such an impression of your home island. Talk about give a dog a bad name.

Yet, you had to acknowledge that there was a real problem in place. Indeed, such was the extent of the problems that two external individuals eventually had to be called in to deal with them. The first was a High Court Judge called Michael Farmer – a Welsh-speaker from Penygroes, across the water in Arfon. Then, several years later, when things had still not improved and the council placed in special measures, a Welsh Assembly member, Carl Sargeant, came in on behalf of the Welsh Government. Carl Sargeant was a burly man who could tell it straight, and he had a huge impact here. Very sadly, he eventually committed suicide in 2019 after being accused of some inappropriate sexual behaviour. That was a hell of a shock and a big loss for Welsh politics, too.

Part of the problem with the council at this stage was so many departures and decisions being passed even though they went against the advice of the council officers. As a councillor myself, I really felt for planning officers such as Wil Evans and Arthur Owen, his successor, seeing so much of their careful advice and guidelines being tossed aside so easily with the councillors passing applications willy-nilly, to all intents and purposes.

And I saw for myself the real nature of the problem when I went on the planning committee, which involved going on visits on a bus to see various locations on the island. It was a real eye-opener, I can tell you! You would be standing on some site or other, listening to the planning officer describing the applications, and then you'd realise that some half a dozen or so of the councillors had disappeared. *Where the hell have they got to?* you would ask yourself, before getting to know later that they had been in the house, discussing terms with the owner! Before long, there were rumours of the brown envelopes being handed out in order to make sure the application was approved.

I never witnessed a brown envelope passing hands personally, but they did appear to be a part of the whole culture of the council at that time. But then, with no paper trail, there was no way that the council's legal officers could do anything about it. I was offered money several times to pass something or other, but I was never tempted to go down that route thankfully. I'm grateful for that strong upbringing of mine and all those years in Elim Chapel, Malltraeth for providing me with a strong moral fibre in that respect.

During my time as a councillor, I made some great friends on the council, with some individuals being a real inspiration for me in terms of learning my craft. One of these was Councillor Goronwy Parry from Valley. As I used to often say – the only good Tory I've ever met!

The only Tory on the council, but a very pleasant and respectable man, who was always ready and willing to offer advice and support to myself at all times. Even when I crossed the floor from the Independents group to join the Plaid Cymru group, this didn't faze Goronwy at all since he always dealt with me as an individual above anything else. I really admired the way he stood his ground in the council chamber, keeping his dignity whatever was happening around him and whatever was being said about him.

He was also very clever in the way he would frame things with his words, with a subtlety often going over the heads of his fellow councillors. I remember being in one meeting when he was tearing a strip off someone or other in that unique way of his and the councillor I was sitting by nudged me and said: "He's really giving it to someone, isn't he?" And I had to tell him: "You do know he's talking about you, don't you?"

It wasn't an easy gig at all for Goronwy Parry, being the only Tory on the county council, but he managed to retain his seat time after time, which showed how much the people of Valley thought of him as their local representative. I've also got place to give thanks to him later as well, since he sent me several very supportive letters while I faced the hardest period of my life – when I was accused of fraud by the Post Office and was eventually imprisoned by them.

Another councillor I had a high regard for came from the other end of the political spectrum entirely, which shows, I hope, that I have an open mind politically and that I am able to relate to people with differing views. This was Councillor Jimmy O'Toole from Holyhead. Although he was nominally a Labour councillor, he tended to keep his distance from the Labour mob who ran Holyhead. Jimmy certainly had his own take on things and was never shy of expressing his opinions in a blunt and forthright way at all times! Sometimes that could cost him.

I remember one night coming out of a county council meeting in Llangefni and Jimmy asking me when the next bus home to Holyhead would be. His Labour colleagues from Holyhead had taken offence at something he said and had gone back without him! I offered him a lift back in my car and I was given chapter and verse about the Labour Party in my ears all the way to Holyhead and for another half an hour outside his house on top of all that! Jimmy was very thankful for that good turn and was always ready to help me with matters relating to Gaerwen after that.

One other time, I was in a housing committee with the housing director, John Arthur Jones, discussing what to do concerning providing housing for a family of Irish people who had just landed in the port. "Send them back to Ireland," said Jimmy. "We've got too many Irish in Holyhead already"– and Jimmy an Irishman himself, of course!

Morawelon, the biggest council estate in Holyhead, was Jimmy's home ground. He was very loyal to his people there and they were just as loyal to him as well. You could describe him as a bit of a 'rough diamond'. It appears that one Labour MP for the island at the time, Cledwyn Hughes, was slightly concerned about what Jimmy would say to people on the doorstep when canvassing at election times. Therefore, he persuaded Jimmy from not venturing to some of the more upmarket areas in the town, lest it damage his campaign! "It's better that you focus on Morawelon for me, Jimmy," would be his message every time. "That's where your people are."

One of the highlights of my time on the county council was to be made chair of the Environmental Health Committee between 2002 and 2006. I was very fortunate to have Grant Shaw as the Council's Chief Environmental Officer, since he was so willing to provide advice and guidance from the very start. When I started, he told me, "Now you're the bloody chair, you've got to bloody well see what we do here!" And he kept to his word as well, providing many hands-on opportunities for me. I'm very thankful since it really helped me to understand and appreciate the importance of the department's work.

There was one significant development in the environmental health field in my own community, as it happens, with the arrival of the Halal Meat Factory. This was a major development for Gaerwen, as it employed some 350 people at one stage, becoming one of the major employers on the island. The owner of Halal at the time was a guy called Mr Ali and he was very keen for me to see everything that when on at the factory. I used to call him 'I want' since he would invariably start each sentence with "I want…"

For some reason, I think he believed I had much more clout on the council that I had in reality and that I was the one in charge of many things that went on there. I was invited all the time to different events at Halal and he also used to phone regularly at night as well. Quite often, when the phone rang around 11pm, I'd hear Eira, my wife, saying; "Oh, it's you again, Mr Ali," and I had to shake my head ferociously to indicate I was not available!

One time, I asked Mr Ali about the lack of Welsh language signs on the site, seeing that Gaerwen was a very Welsh-speaking area. "You find me more Welsh workers, Noel, and I will put up more Welsh signs for you," was his instant response. He was referring to the fact that there were a large number of Polish workers working at the factory at the time, suggesting they were much more willing to work there than many local Welsh people. He made a fair point.

At one stage, Halal had no fewer than fourteen health officers at the site itself as the animal-killing operation was so large-scale. At first, they were slaughtering cattle at the site, around 5,000 every week, but, after the BSE story and then the Foot and Mouth fiasco in 2000, they changed track and went more towards slaughtering lamb. If anything, the operation became even larger with this change of direction, with some 25,000 lambs being slaughtered there every week.

In addition, a thriving packing business also came into being on the site as much of the lamb was packed to be sold to the ASDA supermarket. Halal was an important employer, sustaining some many local families, so when it closed in 2014, it proved to be a big blow for the community. It was also a blow to local farmers as well, as they now had to carry their animals to be slaughtered in places much further away.

I think Llanybydder is the only slaughterhouse in Wales itself, with another one in Ellesmere over the border being the next nearest, which is a very sad state of affairs. It's a matter of deep personal regret for me personally that the old Halal site – over thirty acres of land in Gaerwen – has still not been put to alternative use. There is something very wrong with a state of affairs that allows such a central and convenient site in the middle of the village to be left empty, especially considering that the job market for the young people of the area is so poor at present.

One other development that took place during my time on the Environmental Health Committee was the idea of developing the Ynys Môn coastal path. The path has now become a valuable resource used by local people and visitors alike: 120 miles around the island, all in all. Quite an achievement and I am very glad to have played a part in its development, especially as I'm such a big fan of walking for both your mental health and your physical health in life. It's good to see that much money from the Welsh Government and European funding has been channelled into the development of the coastal path over the past few years. Not many jobs have been created as a direct result of the development, but there can be no doubt it has improved the natural environment on the island and given people an opportunity to keep fit and see more of their own area at the same time. We are so lucky to live on such a beautiful island and I give thanks for that on a daily basis.

During this period, the question of Wylfa B – a new nuclear station on the island – raised its head again. I don't have any issue with the idea of nuclear power as such, but I was worried – and

I'm still worried – about the creation of nuclear weapons, which is associated with all this unfortunately. And then, of course, you have the whole problem of what to do with the waste created, which has still not been answered properly, from what I can see. There was a recent report in a daily newspaper saying that the bill for burying nuclear waste from any new nuclear station in Wales amounts to some £350 million. That's a bill that could sink any idea of an Independent Wales before it got off the ground, which is a real headache, to be honest.

I remember being in a committee once when plans for Wylfa B were being discussed and the developers saying they wanted to bury the waste on Mynydd Parys – an old copper site on the island – as the shafts there went down so deep, to the sea itself in some places. Of course, the talk of Wylfa B has disappeared now, but there is some talk of building some small modular nuclear reactors and we'll see what comes of that.

There's also the issue of who the electricity is being created for, as Wales currently produces twice as much electricity as it needs for its own needs. It would appear once again that Wales is being used to serve England's interests and not her own interests. An old, old story, I'm afraid!

To go back to Mynydd Parys. It's very interesting to note that the Anglesey Mining Company have announced they want to restart their operations there. Their Annual Report for 2022 said they were very happy with the prospects for mining for copper and other minerals on the site, including lithium, which is apparently very plentiful there. Lithium, of course, is very important for producing batteries for electric cars, which are becoming so popular nowadays. It would be good to think that such a development could create new jobs in Amlwch and the area, which is in such dire need of new economic opportunities for its young people – and people of all ages, if it comes to that.

I've long stopped being a county councillor, but I'm still very interested in what's going on here in different ways. The current economic situation on the island is dire and I'm really worried about what the future holds for our young people here. There doesn't seem to be much to keep them here anymore. Yes, of course, life in other big cities like Cardiff, Liverpool and London are more accessible for young people nowadays – much more so than when I was growing up. Even so, I'm sure young people would love to stay or even come back to Ynys Môn if there were better employment opportunities here for them. I've got two grandchildren at university right now, so – considering their own futures – this is something that is very close to my heart.

Going back to the county council situation for a moment, it's very gratifying to see the county council's reputation is now much better under the leadership of the Plaid Cymru group, who have gained control of the council over recent years. They have a young woman, Llinos Medi, as their leader and I'm very proud of the work she has done to improve things within the council over the past few years. We can now hold our heads up high as islanders once again after all the scandals and bad press that came our way for so many years. No more of these 'corruption island' barbs from people!

I think my stint as a county councillor helped me to develop listening skills, the ability to weigh up decisions and the ability to ask relevant questions to myself and to other people as well.

I think, as well, that I came to understand people at a deeper level, understand what drove people, and their motivations at different levels. All that and also being able to change my opinion on situations when the facts changed. As somebody once said: "I, sir, change my mind when the facts change. What do you do?"

Funnily enough, I was offered an opportunity to become a councillor again in 2021. It was an honour to be offered such an opportunity again after being out of it for fifteen plus years after what happened to me with the Post Office. But I decided not to take up the offer since I had so much on my plate trying to settle compensation matters with the Post Office. And besides, so much of the county council's work is now done by, what I call, the *hyrdi gyrdi* ('gadgets') – tablets and mobile phones and the like. I would be lost having to negotiate with these!

I was also able to deepen the connections with my native island when I became a sub-postmaster at Gaerwen in 1991. Eira and I had already had some experience of this nature as we had run the smaller Post Office at Malltraeth for a few years, but the move to Gaerwen was a welcome new challenge for the two of us and a very timely one as well, in view of the fact that the village was growing at that time. It had a new industrial estate with all kinds of businesses setting up there, so it proved to be a very good move for us as a family.

My children, Sian, Arfon and Edwin, soon settled quickly at the local school and within a couple of years we had become part and parcel of the local community. Running the Post Office was an opportunity to put my people skills to good use again and talking to customers every day – in a new capacity now. Of course, I did miss the companionship and camaraderie of my fellow postmen in Llangefni, having enjoyed working alongside them for so many years, but I very quickly adapted to the new situation.

I was lucky having Eira working alongside me, since we were able to support each other in learning the ropes of a new and larger business. Eira also ran a small card shop within the Post Office, which was quite successful in itself, so it was a good and thriving time for us as a family.

From 1991 to 2005, the business built up exponentially and at one point we were taking around £100,000 a week in takings. You see, the Post was the central point for so many transactions for people at that time: pensions, giro, savings, as well as the usual television licence and driving licence business as well. The more the business grew, the more I was paid and by the start of the 2000s, I was earning a salary of £30,000 a very good salary on the island by anybody's standards.

One of the things that helped the business along was the fact that I made a point of trying to help a number of local businesses.

Indeed, one of them, Huws Gray – a builders' merchants – has grown to be one of the largest firms in the whole of north Wales, with expanding interests in parts of England.

I remember, at one stage, I managed to persuade John Llew and Terry Roberts, the joint directors of Huws Gray at the time, not to spend a lot of money on buying an expensive franking machine. I told them that we at the Post Office would take on the task of placing stamps on all their letters and parcels, which were to be delivered all over Wales and the UK. You would then see myself, Eira and Sian of an evening, spending hours placing stamps on correspondence on the kitchen table at the back of the Post Office! It paid off for Huws Gray and for us as well, because they were then doing much more business with us in general.

The work of a postmaster involved long hours, including after-hours work of all sorts, as people would often turn up at the doorstep after 6pm asking for help with something or other. I must have signed many things for people on that kitchen table over the years, including some divorce papers along the way! All in all, these were very fruitful years for myself and the family. Little did we know that our world was about to be turned upside down – ironically enough, thanks to a company located on the other side of the world.

You see, in 1998, a year after he was elected PM, Tony Blair announced an 'IT revolution' and part of that revolution was to introduce a new electronic service for all Post Offices in the UK. He promised at the time that this new system – Horizon – which was to be introduced by the big Japanese company, Fujitsu, would make the system work better for everybody – postmasters and customers alike. However, as we came to see in other ways with Tony Blair, his promises were often based on soundbites alone, with very little reality belonging to them.

Up until that time, the balancing up in the post was done manually every Wednesday at the Post Office. Part of my contract involved ensuring that all the monies had to be balanced on a weekly basis. This worked very well since Eira would always have a look over my initial calculations, lest I made any miscalculations, and this process would take some hours every early Wednesday evenings. These would then be sent to be ratified by the Post Office in Bangor and all the audits we had at that time, both internal and external, were always fine.

Now, though, we were moving to a whole new system where everything would be calculated electronically. I attended one training course over the water at Llanberis, where I was the youngest postmaster there. Indeed, I got to know later that many of those at that meeting decided to retire rather than having to go over to a brand-new system.

Looking back now, I often wish that I would have taken the same course of action… but then again, you can never tell in which direction life is going to take you. And perhaps it's good that we don't know what lies ahead for us in life.

CHAPTER 4

The Accusing

From this point onwards, we will hear a new voice in *The Stamp of Innocence* tale, namely the voice of Sian Thomas, Noel's daughter. Over the years, Sian has played a pivotal role in her father's battle for justice, almost taking on a representative role on behalf of the whole family, and affectionately dubbed the 'home secretary' by her father for all her hard work. Even today, seventeen years on, she is still very much involved in the whole campaign as the public inquiry proceeds this year.

We will now alternate between Noel's voice and Sian's voice in reporting the story. Combining both of their takes on things allows us to take a holistic view of the whole situation.

Noel
It all kicked off on Thursday 13th October 2005.

I opened the Post Office in Gaerwen as per usual that morning, but at 7.30am, two people came to the door, introducing themselves as local auditors. This might sound odd, but, in one sense, it came as a big relief. You see, I had been having some accounting problems with the Post's computerised accounts system for some time.

"Yes, I know," were my first words to them on the doorstep that morning.

"There's some money missing, isn't there?"

I gave them the figure I thought was in question.

The two then asked me to shut the Post for a while so that we could go into the house for a chat. I showed them into the kitchen and asked what the extent of the problem actually amounted to.

"Well, there is a definite problem with the accounts," said one of them. "And there is a large sum of money missing here."

"How much money exactly?" I asked.

"£52,000," responded one of the two.

Even though I knew there was a problem and had actually acknowledged this when answering the door to them, my heart sank when I heard this figure and I had to sit down on the sofa in complete shock.

I then asked If I could let Eira, my wife, and Sian, my daughter, know about the situation and Eira was allowed to phone Sian at her workplace and tell her to come home at once as we had a big problem on our hands.

With Eira herself also in such a state, it was surprising that she was able to use the phone at all, to be honest, but she managed to do so and Sian came over immediately. Auntie Gwenda, Eira's twin and a big part of our family, also came over to the house to see if she could help out in any way, after she was informed about what was going on.

I'd barely had a chance to explain what had happened to the two of them when there was another knock on the door. Two Post Office Investigators from Warrington this time. One of them, a female, wasted no time at all: "Where's the money?" she barked at me. "What have you done with the missing £52,000?" almost before she had introduced herself.

She wanted to interview me on my own, but my family said no and thankfully she gave up on that idea one hearing that.

"I haven't touched any of the money," I responded, trying to hold it together and appear as firm as I could, even though my voice was shaking and my whole world was crumbling all around me.

The auditors then explained that they had conducted two audits in the post that morning, with both of them showing that £52,000 was missing. They had then asked another local sub-postmaster, Jim Evans from Llanfairpwll, to come and run the post in my place. As things turned out, he only lasted around half an hour since he discovered he was down £100 almost immediately. He then said on the spot that he did not want to continue since there was too much risk involved for him. So, the Post Office was shut indefinitely – an early sign for everyone in the community that there was something very dodgy going on.

The next step in the saga was for a police car to draw up outside and two police officers then stepped into the lounge, which was already quite full that morning.

"Cuff him!" commanded the female auditor from Liverpool immediately, but, as it happened, Gwenda, my sister-in-law, knew the police officer and had a quiet word in his ear. I also knew him. And fair play to him, he refused to place the cuffs on my wrists.

However, this didn't deter the female auditor from Liverpool at all, who was really hitting her stride with things by now. She announced that I was being arrested for theft and that I would have to accompany them to the police station in Holyhead.

And this is what would have happened, but for Sian's intervention – pleading for us all to have lunch together first and then she would drive me over to Holyhead first thing in the afternoon. Surprisingly, the aggressive auditor agreed to this request.

And there we were, the whole family together in a state of shock – myself, Eira, Gwenda, Arfon, Sian and Edwin. We tried to eat some ham sandwiches, if I remember correctly, only they were totally tasteless that lunchtime, almost like paper in our mouths.

"I haven't stolen a penny!" I told them in a flood of tears, almost not able to get the words out at all.

The ensuing family group hug in our kitchen that day gave me the confidence to know from the start that the family would have my back whatever happened. Fortunately, for me, this solidarity has remained throughout the saga over the whole seventeen years, and has been something to sustain me and encourage me despite everything that has taken place.

The rest of that day, 13th October 2005, was just a complete blur. We arrived at Holyhead after lunch and it was there that I spent the rest of the day up until the early hours of the next day. This proved to be an incredibly tedious and frustrating experience for me, since I had to wait for my solicitor to arrive before starting any form of defence and that literally meant hours and hours just sitting there with all kinds of thoughts swirling about in my head.

I was also starting to realise that although I was actually sitting in a police station in Holyhead, it was the auditors themselves who were asking the questions – not the police – on behalf of the Post Office. The police, incredibly, weren't part of the process at all! You see, the Post Office had the right to conduct their own prosecution procedure, with no need for any input from the police or even the Crown Prosecution service!

This incident in the police station in Holyhead was an early sign of all the power and authority embedded within the Post Office, who were to destroy my life and the lives of so many others over the years to come.

When my solicitor, Eilian Williams, eventually arrived in a few hours, his advice to me was to say, "No Comment," to everything that was asked of me. As you can imagine, the next few hours were not very productive.

To be honest, I was completely numb throughout it all, just trying to process everything, but not able to do it. My mind was just a racing whirl of thoughts one after the other.

After what seemed to be an eternity, I was released and Sian came to fetch me in the car. It was around 2am when I reached my bed, but I didn't sleep a wink all night.

In one day, my life and the life of my whole family had been turned upside down entirely and I knew things would never be the same for me or my family. I was a husband, a father, a grandfather, a postmaster and a councillor, but it was as if all those roles had been taken away from me in an instant. And I was now nothing – a non-person, in effect.

I would wake the following morning having to face life as someone who had been accused of stealing £52,000 from the business I had been running for twelve years, knowing full well that the Post Office in Gaerwen had already been closed and that the story about why it was closed already going like wildfire throughout the community and the wider area.

Being someone who always enjoyed working and meeting people every day, the idea of not being able to do that anymore was almost too much to handle. I still find it difficult to this day, to describe how dreadful that feeling was, but I can state with no uncertainty at all that the next year was going to be the most difficult of my life.

Sian

The morning that Dad was arrested, I was working at AO Roberts Builders in Gaerwen, my home village. I had a phone call from my mam, shouting and screaming, saying something terrible had happened to my dad and I needed to come home at once.

"What's wrong? What's wrong?" I kept asking.

"I can't tell you over the phone, but your dad is in a hell of a pickle here. Come home immediately."

I ran upstairs to ask my boss for some time off and drove home in a blind panic, without a clue what was about to face me. When I walked into the kitchen, Mam was crying her eyes out at the sink.

"What's happened? What's going on?" I remember shouting at her.

All my mam could say was a mumbled, "Your dad," with a nod towards the living room next door.

When I stepped into the living room, Dad was sitting on the sofa with three strangers standing around him. "What's up, Dad? What on earth is going on here?" I asked him.

My dad looked at me with an incredibly pained look on his face, before saying, almost in a whisper; "These auditors are saying I've stolen £52,000 from the Post."

Well, I was in a state of complete shock hearing this and my Auntie Gwenda, who was also in the room, tried to say something to reassure me.

"Don't you speak that language in front of me," one of the three auditors snapped at her.

This totally enraged me and I still don't know how I managed to stop myself from giving her a real earful for being so disrespectful towards my language.

The female auditor kept repeating, "What has he done with the money? You must know what he's done with it. C'mon, don't make things difficult for us." All this in an incredibly aggressive, in-your-face manner.

Her questions kept bouncing around in my mind all day. They were still there, hours later, when we drove to Holyhead to fetch my dad after he was released from police custody in the early hours of the following morning.

Questions, questions, questions; this would be my life and the life of the whole family from this point onwards.

Noel

The next three months were a complete nightmare. Back and forth from various courts – Llangefni, Caernarfon, Mold – around eight times in all as the case moved forward at a snail's pace.

I had been led to understand that 'Theft' and 'False Accounting' were the charges being levelled against me and that £52,000 was the sum in question. Yet this figure was not mentioned at all in the various court hearings I had to attend. It was always just a case of turning up, confirming my name and address, and that was it until the next time – 'deferred' until the next hearing since things were not quite ready, with no opportunity for me to say anything really. And despite the fact that six Post Office solicitors turned up every time, all in their Savile Row suits, they never said anything in essence either!

It was just a totally frustrating process, since you were not any closer to the shore after every single appearance in court. I just had to learn to accept the situation as the solicitors kept telling me that all the relevant details of the case would eventually be heard during the final hearing in the county court. As we will see shortly, I was very naive to believe all this and to accept all of these legal protocols as if they were some kind of gospel, trusting that one day there would be an opportunity to argue my case and prove to everyone that I was innocent and that I hadn't stolen a single penny. Unfortunately, I came to realise very quickly the truth of that old saying of Lord Denning's: 'The law is an ass'.

The most difficult aspect of this long and frustrating process over so many months was not being able to work. And having to find ways of filling the long hours during every day as I had been suspended by the Post Office from my duties. I have worked every day of my life and not being able to do that was like prison in itself. Prison before prison, as things turned out.

Another heartbreaker for me was having to face people in the community after the story was plastered across the media and in the local newspapers, such as the *Holyhead and Anglesey Mail*, the *Daily Post* and the like. Having always sought to live a good life and serve my community as a postmaster and councillor, it was as if all this service was now under suspicion, both past and present.

A couple of really unpleasant incidents took place during this time as well. At one point, I was in a local supermarket when somebody shouted, "Lock the doors! The thief has landed." Usually, though, people didn't say anything to my face, but then one was always worried about what they were really thinking and what was being said about me behind my back.

One was also being disappointed in other directions. I had served as the secretary of the Gwynedd Sub-postmasters between 2002 and 2004, but when asked if the federation could help me in the situation I faced, the secretary at the time turned round and said: "If you've been caught with your hands in the till, I can't help you."

This unhelpful and almost hostile attitude was to be repeated time and time again over the next decade or so with the federation shown to be a toothless tiger – an organisation funded by the Post Office and in its pocket, to all intents and purposes. All I could do in these situations was to try and keep my head high and hope that somehow everything would come to light eventually and I would be cleared in time.

My conscience was totally clear. I knew I had not stolen any money at all. My family also knew that I hadn't stolen any money. Even though I was earning a decent salary by 2006, we lived a very modest life as a family and I drove a old Saab for a car. I also had a fair inkling of what had gone wrong in the whole situation: the new Horizon computerised accounting system that had been brought in by the Post Office in 2000.

As I mentioned earlier, before that date all the accounts were performed manually and Eira and myself had a good system in place to do this between ourselves for some hours every Wednesday afternoon. We would then send these on to the Post Office in Bangor that evening for final verification.

As mentioned, the Horizon computerised accounting system was introduced in 2000 with the then PM Tony Blair boasting that this system would transform the service for everyone, customers and sub-postmasters alike. However, like everything else with Tony Blair, there was a huge difference between the words that came out of his mouth and what was actually delivered. Several times, I would come down to the office in the middle of the night, unable to sleep, and see the computerised system making a noise and a number of figures appearing on the screen and then changing in front of my eyes. Now, I'm not computer-savvy at all, and all I could think at the time was that the system was rebooting itself. But the truth of the matter is that it was all the bugs in the system that were playing up and causing merry havoc within the system – as shown by the clear inconsistencies that were coming to light by this time.

In 2003, an audit showed we were £6,000 out as far as our figures were concerned. On this occasion, the system actually showed we had £6,000 less than was there in reality. With this particular problem, we came to an agreement that the Post Office would pay £3,000 and I would pay £3,000 to clear the discrepancy. I wasn't happy at all that this had to be done, but then it was part of my contract as a sub-postmaster that the figures had to balance on a weekly basis, so I had no option but to accept the Post Office's offer.

We then had successful audits in 2004 and 2005 and I was hopeful that the teething problems with the system were now being cleared up. But then, at the end of 2005, there were imbalances cropping up all the time and I had to make regular calls to the Post's helpline in Rotherham in the north of England to ask them for assistance.

I must have phoned them at least a dozen times in 2005, recording each one of these calls on a calendar I had in the Post itself. The advice I got from the individuals manning the helpline was always the same: "Roll it over to next week. The system will correct itself. Don't worry." But because of the fact that these had to balance correctly every single week, I had to plug any discrepancies between the money in the Post and the money showing up on the system – from my own pocket – or lose my job. I had to take a few bank loans to finance all this, in the vain hope that the system would eventually self-correct as the helpline kept telling me.

Looking back now, I am so angry with myself that I accepted what they were telling me and that I didn't challenge these discrepancies more forcibly. But then again, I had no idea at the time that this was happening on a much larger scale, with others not challenging it either, so I try not to blame myself too much.

I also realise I was up against the queen herself in one sense – i.e. the Royal Mail and all the power, influence and money the company had in bringing a case against one small sub-postmaster. What hope did I, a mere islander from Wales, have in such a situation?

Sian

It was incredibly difficult for us as a family to be able to deal with what had happened to Dad, especially as we all knew he was totally innocent. I thought the world of him and he had always been there for me all over the years. Whatever problem I had, I knew I could always turn to Dad for help.

I didn't doubt him for one second. I know that I'm totally biased as his own daughter, but – quite truthfully – you'll never find anyone as honest and true as my dad. The very idea that Dad had stolen £52,000 from the customers he knew so well in Gaerwen and from the employers he had worked for an unbroken forty-two years was totally bonkers. Yet we all had to face the public who had been bombarded with this story by the media – the television, the radio, the *Daily Post* and local papers.

To be honest, I have come to consider the media and the way it can shape and drive people's opinions so easily in a very different way now. I've become very media-sceptic, you could say, after what I saw. Seeing all this, perhaps I don't blame some people so much for turning against Dad, but, at the time itself, it was very, very difficult for me.

We had people banging on the door late at night and shouting nasty insults. I also came across people shouting abuse at me on the street. On one occasion, a woman I knew came up to me on a street in Gaerwen and put her face right next to mine, saying: "Shame on you!" This really shook me, I can tell you.

We lost friends and other friends kept their distance. That year, from the time Dad was arrested and accused to the final court hearing was a complete nightmare for us all. I wasn't able to sleep, I wasn't eating properly and I had to take time out from work, but I had to be strong for Dad's sake and the rest of the family as well.

It was also terribly hard on Mam having to deal with all of this and trying to comfort my dad, who had, quite naturally, gone into a very depressed state. Quite often, I had to come over to Gaerwen from my home in Malltraeth to help out, and to try and sustain everyone's spirits the best I could. This was a constant strain on me throughout that year as all of us tried to wrack our brains to try and work out what had happened. Where the hell had that money got to? Where exactly was the missing £52,000? Poor dad was torturing himself more than any one of us, trying to figure things out.

I've lost count of the times we had the conversation with Dad, going through all of the details and what we could remember. But every single time, the only answer we could arrive at – the only answer that made any sense to any one of us – was that it was Horizon, the Post Office's IT system, which was at fault. Somehow, that system had miscalculated how much money was in the Post and had made the actual balance itself appear to be much less than it was.

It was one thing to come to that realisation ourselves. It was another matter entirely to be able to explain that to other people. It was just too difficult to explain somehow. We just had to hope, against hope, that some new information would come to light – information that would clear dad's name and that we, as a family, would be able to wake from this hellish nightmare we had found ourselves in.

But the days turned into weeks and the weeks into months, and there was no sign of anything turning up. Nothing at all.

Noel
The months were rolling by, but nothing seemed to be happening at all and I have to admit my spirits were very low at this point. Not being able to work was such an alien experience for me, and losing

the pattern and consistency of going to the Post every morning and dealing with my customers was a hell of a shock to the system.

It must have been so difficult for Eira and the rest of the family to have to deal with me during this period of time. Everything seemed to be against me. On the whole, the people in the area were okay with me to my face, but, even so, things weren't as they used to be and everybody seemed to be keeping me at arm's length somehow. This was so difficult for me being someone who loves to chat with people and have fun with people and so on.

Christmas always used to be a joyous and fun-filled experience in our household, but none of us was in any kind of mood to be able to enjoy Christmas 2005 because of this black cloud above my head and the worry and anxiety about what lay ahead for us as a family in 2006.

Each week, I would ask my solicitor if there was anything new to report, but he had barely anything to tell me. The only information that was given to him by the Post Office was that they had told him I was the only sub-postmaster in this situation and that no one else was in the frame at all. In time, of course, it became clear that this was a complete lie, as the same charges of 'Theft' and 'False Accounting' had been laid against countless other sub-postmasters during this period and later. I was totally oblivious to this at the time and there was no coverage at all in the media either, since these were all small local events and not brought to the attention of a wider UK audience. It was only much later that all of this became public knowledge and the one then became two, half a dozen, dozens and then hundreds. All in all, over seven hundred sub-postmasters would face exactly the same problem over the years to come.

When it came to the issue of defending myself when the final court hearing would eventually take place, there was one big problem that was haunting me at this time – the fact that all the information I had in the Post at the time, and all the dates and times I had contacted the helpline, had all been taken away.

You see, the auditors had performed a complete clean sweep of the Post when I was arrested and had taken every single item with them. Everything. Even every item related to my council work. They had also locked up the Post and the shop. All the stuff that Eira had in the shop went to waste and we just had to give it all away in the end, losing thousands in the process. All the materials from the Post itself were then deposited at the Post Office Building in Bangor. A few months later, I was informed that all of this material had been lost because of a fire in the building – talk about putting salt on the wound! This meant that my defence, in terms of information about the problems I had been experiencing with the system, and all those time I had flagged up these issues, had disappeared entirely. It had literally gone up in flames. This was a complete accident, of course, but the fire had just made my case for the defence so much harder as now I couldn't use the evidence I had collected to show the extent of the IT problems. I could have screamed when I heard about it. How on earth could I defend myself now?

Despite all this, I was trying to hold on to some hope. I kept telling myself that I would have my opportunity to present my case in court and that it would then be up to a jury of ordinary citizens to decide whether I was guilty or not. This hope kept me going through many long, dark nights, I can tell you.

At the time, I didn't know about all the power the Post Office had and the fact that they even had the right to conduct their own prosecutions – that is, the CPS (Crown Prosecution Service), who usually decide if there is a case to bring prosecutions to court, didn't have a role to play in this process whatsoever. So there was no level of neutrality and professional objectivity at play at all. The Post Office would be prosecuting one of their own staff members, under their own rules. Judge, jury and executioner, as things would turn out.

At last, the big day finally arrived: the final hearing in the Caernarfon Crown Court on 13th November 2006. By this point, my solicitor had engaged the services of a barrister to represent me in court and he had been discussing the details of the case back and forth with the Post Office.

On the day itself, I was sitting in the court waiting room, waiting to go into the court, when the barrister came into the room.

"We've been able to reach a plea-bargain arrangement with them," he said.

"They are willing to drop the 'theft' charge, as long as you agree to accept the 'false accounting' charge and make no mention of the Horizon system."

A week previous to all this, we had been informed that no jury would be provided for the case. I have to say that was a hell of knock for me. Hadn't I been waiting, pining even, for months for the opportunity to present my case to a jury and to have everything in the open to be fully discussed at last? But now, not only was there not going to be a jury on the case, but I also had to plead guilty to something I just hadn't done.

Perhaps some of you will be asking: "Well, Noel, why didn't you just plead not guilty, if you didn't do it?"

It's a fair enough question, but you've got to remember that I was under a huge amount of stress and pressure that morning. There was my barrister, with all his experience in the legal world, telling me, in no uncertain terms, that this was the very best option for me to take. Since by accepting the lesser charge, it would mean that I would avoid going to prison. And you also had the whole court protocol and the need to find some speedy resolution also being a huge weight for me to bear.

You really have to be in a situation such as this to realise all the authority and power that people such as barristers and people in the legal system have, and how they can just browbeat ordinary individuals with all this. It really was made plain to me that I had no real choice in the matter whatsoever, and that I would be appearing in front of the judge and pleading guilty to the charge.

Looking back at it all now, it was a huge mistake that I bitterly regret. When I stepped into the court, another huge shock awaited me. They had changed the judge at the very last minute. In every single hearing I had attended during the year, the same judge had been in front of me, a gentleman by the name of Robert Hughes. But now, in the most important and final hearing of them all, there was a completely different judge in place. He was another Welsh speaker, as it happens – Winston Roddick from Caernarfon – who had actually served as the Cwnsler Cenedlaethol in the National Assembly in Cardiff between 1998 and 2003.

As I stood in the dock to face him, he delivered some good news to me initially, by saying that he had received over a hundred letters from individuals testifying to my good character. Indeed, he told me he had never before received so many letters of support in all his time as a judge, and that he was therefore dealing with what he termed a 'huge fall from grace' in the eyes of the public.

If my heart leapt in hearing about that level of public support that had come my way – raising my hopes that this would have an effect upon him – these were soon to be dashed completely, since he then just followed the letter of the law. He asked me how I pleaded to the charge of 'False Accounting'.

"Guilty," I said, expecting that he would at least then give me an opportunity to present my side of things. Hadn't I waited a whole year for this chance? But it wasn't to happen.

"I'm giving you a sentence of nine months for false accounting," said Roddick.

I stood there, expectantly, waiting for the additional 'suspended for a year'.

But those words didn't come from his mouth at all. He just looked at me and said, coldly, "Take him down."

I was then the one to go cold, with a cold sweat breaking out all over me. I looked up at the family in the public gallery to see the complete shock on the faces of Arfon, Edwin, Gail, Sian and Gwenda. No sooner than I had done this, I was being bundled from the dock by the court officers and led to the bottom of the court. I had been sent to jail, for nine months.

Sian

We had been waiting and waiting and waiting for the big day. Mam, Arfon, Edwin, Gail, Auntie Gwenda and myself had been so looking forward for this opportunity to clear Dad's name and bring a year-long nightmare to an end. We all just wanted our lives back. And just wanted to see Dad happy again, doing the thing he enjoyed doing more than anything else in life – serving his customers in the Post and helping the people of Gaerwen as much as he could as a county councillor.

Dad had continued in his role as a councillor during the year, but things were not as they used to be. Less people phoned him, less people called by; it was as if they had accepted he was guilty and didn't want to rely on him anymore. So much for the 'Innocent until proven guilty' idea, which I thought was at the very heart of the legal system here. I know this withdrawal hurt Dad very much, even though he didn't talk about it a lot. Dad is a very private individual and, more often than not, he keeps things to himself, not sharing his thoughts with even Mam herself. It was a very difficult and frustrating state of affairs for all of us, who just wanted to help and support him all we could, and see if there was anything else we could do in the meantime as the court hearing dragged on during the year. But then, I just had to respect the fact that this was his way of dealing with the situation.

From my perspective, I threw myself into things from the very start. You could almost say it took my life over completely in a way – that's how strong the drive was to protect Dad and clear his name. One of the things we managed to do during these months was to employ a forensic accountant out of the legal aid we had been awarded to fight the case against Dad. This forensic accountant then spent some three months digging around the computerised system in the Post and managed to find some cheques and the like that hadn't properly been accounted for in the audit that had been made.

He eventually managed to get the 'missing' sum down from £52,000 to £43,000 by finding a couple of cheques in the system. This gave us hope and raised the possibility that more unaccounted-for items could come to light again. Unfortunately, such individuals are very costly and we ran out of the legal-aid funds. Who knows how much more he would have unearthed if the funds were available, but we will never know this.

I remember 'D Day' – the day of the final hearing in Caernarfon Crown Court as if it was yesterday. Mam decided to stay at home as she just could not face the stress of the whole occasion, but her twin, Auntie Gwenda, who was such an important part of our family, was there along with Arfon, Edwin and his wife, Gail, and myself to support Dad in court.

I'll never forget the barrister coming into the waiting room to announce he had agreed a plea-bargain with the Post, especially as he and I had some form, you could say. You see, he and I had a bit of a to-do in his chambers in Chester a week before the case as he had told me then that there would be no jury for the final hearing. I was absolutely livid hearing this.

"Excuse me," I told him. "Can we just have a private word for a minute?"

We went out of the room and I turned to him, lifted him up with the lapels of his black gown and placed him on the wall behind the two of us.

"Are you bloody joking or what, man?" I said to him in my temper.

He turned a deathly shade of pale.

I then felt someone tapping me on my shoulder, saying, "You had better put him down, Sian." It was another barrister, who happened to be walking by!

Within a few seconds, I was being escorted out of the chamber by two burly security guards. Looking back, I'm not proud of my behaviour that day, but then I was *so* angry with his announcement that there wouldn't be a jury allowed to hear the case. We'd placed all our hopes on having twelve members of the public being able to hear the evidence and come to a rational decision on the whole matter.

The barrister tried to explain to me later that no jury member would be able to understand the case since it was so complex, with no legal precedent in place at all.

"But we've been promised a jury to hear the case – that's what kept us going throughout the whole year," I said. "And why wouldn't members of the public be able to 'understand' the case? Are you suggesting that members of the public are too thick or what?"

I was really wound up about this and seeing stars, to be honest. But what was the use? The system had decided this was the way it was to be and the opinion of Sian Thomas of Gaerwen counted for nothing at all. And when I was then told on the morning of the hearing itself that Dad had to plead guilty to 'False Accounting' as well – well, that was like a red cloth to a bull – or a red cloth to a redhead in my case!

"Why do you have to plead guilty to something you haven't done, Dad?" I asked him. "What sense is in that, for God's sake?!"

Poor Dad looked so confused and lost in the middle of all this. He knew in his heart of hearts he shouldn't accept this guilty plea, but yet he was under so much pressure from the solicitors and the court itself to make some kind of deal work. And there was I, raging inside, just wanting to shake everyone around me about what was about to happen, and shout at everybody: "Wake up! Wake up, all of you! Can't you see how bloody wrong all this is?!"

But everything was stacked against me. What could little old me do in such a situation? It was so frustrating; I just wanted to scream at the unfairness of it all. Perhaps now, a few years down the line, I can be a bit more understanding towards the barrister and realise that he must also have been under tremendous pressure from the court and the Post Office to reach a deal. Everybody was under huge pressure that day. All I could was to pray that the deal that was cut would work and that it would mean that Dad could avoid going to jail. So, we said farewell to Dad and went to sit in the public gallery. We never thought for a second that that would be the last time we would see him for several weeks. Not for a second.

The hearing itself was a complete farce. A sham. A sham of a system. After all the months of waiting, the worry, the trauma for us as a family, it only lasted some five minutes at most. Dad wasn't allowed to say anything in his own defence and despite all the promises that were made, he was sent to prison for nine months. I'll never forget Winston Roddick saying those words: "Take him down." There was something so cruel, so chilling, so final about his words somehow.

And we just had to sit in the public gallery, totally helpless, not able to lift a finger to help Dad at all. All we could do was to look on in absolute horror through our tears as Dad was led down from the dock to the bottom of the court. You won't believe this, but we weren't even allowed to say goodbye to him as it went against the court's 'protocols'. The barrister came up to hand us Dad's coat and his wallet, and it was almost as though he was announcing to us that Dad had died.

So that was it. Dad was on his way to jail and we had no idea where he was even going to. What a beast of a system; breaking not only one individual, but breaking a family, too.

We made the journey back from Caernarfon to Malltraeth on Ynys Môn in a state of complete shock – in complete silence, too. And then, of course, we had to break the news to Mam. That was so incredibly difficult, I can tell you. We decided not to watch the television at all that evening and spent the time trying to comfort each other the best we could under the circumstances, hunched around my coal fire with duvets all around us. The phone kept on ringing, and ringing and ringing, all night long, until around 2am.

As I said, we didn't watch the television coverage of the case that night, but I have seen the footage since. I still have nightmares about the shot of Dad being led from the court in handcuffs to a Securicor van. Despite it all, I'm immensely proud of one fact – a fact that I treasure to this very day. Dad looked straight at the cameras, without trying to hide his gaze in any way.

He knew he had nothing to hide. He had nothing to be ashamed of. We all knew that as well, of course, but we had no idea how long we would have to wait until all the truth came out and how much we would have to suffer as a family before we reached that point.

CHAPTER 5

Life in Prison – Walton and Kirkham

Noel

"Take him down."

Three cold, hard words that still give me nightmares to this very day, years down the line. Nine months, under lock and key.

It came as a huge shock to hear I was to be sent to prison for nine months, when I'd only pleaded guilty to 'False Accounting' in order to avoid prison. That was the whole point – and now my trust had been betrayed. Betrayed by a system I had believed had come up with an acceptable compromise for both sides. But now, only one side had to pay the price for that betrayal.

In the hours following the case at Caernarfon Crown Court, I was in a state of complete shock – in a kind of freeze mode, you could say. I just could not believe that the case had been wrapped up in so little time. How long did it last? Five or ten minutes, at best – and I wasn't allowed to say a word to defend myself. Not a single word. Hadn't I waited and waited and waited for over a year for the opportunity to do that?

All I could do was stand in the dock, feeling I'd been stripped completely bare for all the world to see – in all my shame and all my hurt.

What made things so much worse for me was the fact that I was unable to share how I felt at the time with anyone at all, since none of my family were allowed to come and see me before I left the court. I wasn't even allowed to say goodbye to them before leaving them for nine long months.

On top of all the shock, of course, I felt an immense amount of anger that the system had let me down so badly. And let my family down so badly, too. Little did I know at the time that this 'letting down' was to be a constant theme in my life for many years from that point onwards. Sometimes, it's a relief that we don't know what's ahead of us in life.

Originally, I was supposed to be taken to Altcourse – that was what I was told at the start. Somebody mentioned to me, "It's not too bad there, you know," as Altcourse is a more modern, open prison apparently. It turned out to be a never-ending journey in that white Securicor van from Caernarfon that day. It stopped countless times on its journey along the coast to pick up more people who had been sent to jail. As the van made its way towards its eventual destination, more and more of the individual units on the van where we were placed were being filled up as well.

It became obvious to me that this was not the first time that many of those on board had been on this journey. I saw several knowing looks being exchanged between some of them, as if they knew full well what lay ahead, while I felt out of it completely, without a clue about what was likely to face me at the end of the journey.

And when we reached Securicor's centre in Prestatyn, the second bad news of the day was delivered. There was no space in Altcourse, after all, as it was full. Instead, I was being sent to Walton in Liverpool. I didn't know at the time, but Walton was among one of the oldest and most poorly maintained prisons throughout the whole of Britain. It was a huge place, able to hold some 850 inmates, but, despite its size, it had been allowed to deteriorate over a number of years without any real improvements made to it at all.

It was well past midnight when we eventually reached Walton that evening and the two first experiences that came my way gave me a good idea about what was ahead of me in this prison. I got served some cold chips after arriving and – although I hadn't had any food since the morning – they were totally tasteless and made me feel quite ill. After, I had to take a shower. And not any old shower, mind – oh no. A shower taken in front of some of the prison's officers, all three of them, as if they took great pleasure in watching this humiliation of the new inmate. I came to understand later that this was exactly the purpose of the exercise.

The two experiences seemed to be telling me from the off that this is how you will be treated in here. Like dirt. And you might as well get used to that from the start, mate.

After the humiliating shower, I had to change from my own clothes to the prison uniform, which was a green jersey and some scruffy blue jeans, and receive my own prison number just as if I was a sheep being prepared for the sale. Then, I was led through a series of different doors, which were opened and shut in turn, and was taken up to a cell on the third floor of this huge prison.

Stepping into the cell, I met Ian, from Birkenhead, with whom I would be sharing my personal space for the next nine months. I just stood there, looking around the small, spare cell, with its two plain bunks and a toilet space at the back of the cell. Looking up, I could see the rain coming in from a hole in a window, which had been placed high up on the far wall of the cell.

I had just endured the worst day of my life, but I sensed that there was worse, much worse, to come. And then it hit me like a thunderbolt. After my time in Paradwys ('Paradise') as a young postman, I had now been thrown to the pits of hell. And nine months of this hell lay ahead of me.

Sian

As I said earlier, the worst thing about the whole experience in court in Caernarfon that day was not being able to say goodbye to Dad before he was taken from us. Hearing the judge's words that morning was bad enough, like a knife through the heart, but it was then rubbing salt in the wound for us all as a family to be prevented from even seeing Dad afterwards – because of the court's 'protocols'. We weren't even able to give him a hug before he was taken away in that bloody white van.

Over the years, I've thought a lot about that day, and what I come back to time and time again is the sheer cruelty of such a system – how inhumane it is to be able to do that, not only to one human being, but to his family as well. Unfortunately, that was just a foretaste of what was to come. The system was to ramp up its cruelty to even more unimaginable levels.

For two whole weeks, we simply had no idea where Dad had been taken. No idea at all. No information about where he was or how he was either. We phoned our solicitor in desperation every single day and his response was the same every time – he had no idea where Dad was either. It's not too much of an exaggeration to say that we were close to losing our minds at this time. It's still hard today to fully describe our feelings. Even today, it still hurts like hell. I just can't believe they were able to do this to Dad and to us a family as well.

On top of all this, after the court hearing, no one offered any kind of help to us as a family or any kind of guidance of any sort. We were just left in a complete state of confusion, as if the system was telling us: 'Suck it up – you are going to be part of this punishment as well.' Torture added to torture, punishment added to punishment, cruelty added to cruelty – for all of us.

As a family, we weren't able to sleep, we weren't able to eat – we were not functioning in any way really. It was like a permanent nightmare, which we were unable to wake from. I still don't know how we got through all this, to be honest.

It was a full two weeks before a letter arrived from Dad from Walton Prison, Liverpool. He had actually written the letter straight after arriving at Walton, but there were some initial difficulties as the prison was unwilling to allow Welsh language letters to be processed, which was a disgrace in itself, of course, but it also meant we had to wait even longer for the letter to arrive. Somehow, I'm not sure how, the problem was eventually resolved and the original Welsh language letter arrived in our home.

At last! At long last, we knew where Dad was. I can't begin to tell you how much of a relief that was for us all as a family. We cried a whole bucketful of tears that morning when the letter came through the letter box – it was as if an immense weight had been lifted off all our shoulders.

Not only had we had to cope with the fact that Dad had been sent to prison and deal with local people in the wake of that fact, but we had been completely in the dark as to where he was and, even more importantly, *how* he was.

My main worry throughout all this was how Dad would be able to cope with the experience of being in prison. I didn't share this with other members of the family at the time, but I must admit that I did consider whether Dad would come through the experience of being in prison for nine months at all, being such a pure and honest soul, and someone who was so much a family man as well. The idea of Dad being under lock and key in Walton was a permanent nightmare for me; an anxiety and fear that never left me, day or night.

That was why that first letter was something to treasure, to hold on to so tightly. I don't know how many times I picked up that letter from Walton as a kind of lifeline for us all, to be read and reread time and time again.

A few days letter, another letter arrived from Walton. This time, Dad had included a pink 'permission to visit' form for us to fill in and send back. This letter also informed us that Dad had now been transferred from Walton to Kirkham Prison near Preston. We sent the form back immediately and started to organise our visit to Kirkham. This visit would take place three weeks after he was initially sent down. We were going to see him again! Hallelujah!

Noel

Those first few days in Walton was like a living hell for me. There's no other way to describe it, to be honest.

The worst thing about it all was the fact that I was being locked up for twenty-three hours a day in the cell as if I was some kind of rabbit in a cage. It's hard for me to explain how difficult that was for me and, looking back, it's hard to believe I came through it, in a way.

I was only allowed an hour a day to leave the cell to go down three levels to the canteen for breakfast, lunch and supper, and carry the meals back up the stairs to the cell. As there was nothing else to do for twenty-three hours a day, there was nothing to be done but lie down on the bunk with my eyes fixed on the clock on the opposite wall, watching it going by so slowly, hour by hour. The clock seemed to be part of the punishment. Tick-tock, tick-tock – the hands of the clock looked as if they were not moving at all – and me just wanting to scream out in frustration and despair at it all.

And the constant rehashing of thoughts, of course. Oh yes, there was a constant whirl of repetitive and negative thoughts going on, believe you me. And what exactly was I thinking about during this time? Good question. Where do I start with this? Well, it was just a complete mish-mash of thoughts, to be honest, one after the other. No peace from these thoughts. No peace at all.

In the first place, I felt this immense sense of shame having landed in such a place. Shame for myself, shame for my family and shame for my community to have been drawn into such a scandal. Then blaming myself for having accepted the deal that the barrister and the Post Office had cobbled together. There was a lot of that going on, for sure. Then, *Bloody hell, Noel! Why didn't you make more of a fuss about all those problems that came up on that IT system?! Why hadn't I told the Post Office that I wasn't willing to go on until those problems were sorted out?*

There was no end to the self-critical voice in my head. I was beating myself up 24/7. Then waves of terror and blind panic would break over me that there were nine months of this ahead of me. And of course, a very, very heavy heart thinking about my poor family at home. As bad as it was for me in here, it was my family that had to face the public and a whole community back home after what had happened. It was them that had to deal with all of that on a day-to-day basis. How would poor Eira cope with all this? How would Arfon, Edwin and Sian cope? And Auntie Gwenda as well, who was also such a central part of our family.

And then I worried about all the customers in the Post in Gaerwen. The people I had been dealing with on a day-to-day basis for years. What would happen to all of them now that the Post had closed? What a complete shitshow it was all round.

It was enough to send someone into a state of depression and I'm ready enough to admit that I found myself in a very dark place at this time. I felt really, really low on a constant basis. Not able to sleep, tossing and turning in my bunk, and having to listen to the shouts and screams from the other cells and people banging on their cell doors all night long. These antics every night brought it home to me that not only had I landed in hell, but that the devils were also here, all around me. And as I was unable to sleep properly each night, it was a case of reliving everything that had happened to me, with the same question coming up time and time again throughout the long hours: *Where did that bloody money go? Where the hell is it? Think, man, think!*

The only thing that allowed me to get through all this, really, was Ian – the lad from Birkenhead, who shared the cell with me. Ian was a bit of a jailbird, for sure, and was quite obviously very familiar with the experience of spending time in Walton. You could almost say it was like a second home for him. I'm convinced that sharing a cell with such a character was a blessing from above for me. God only knows how things would have turned out if I had been in that cell myself. Mind you, he didn't believe me for a moment when I told him I was totally innocent of stealing the £52,000. "I would have liked to have a figure like that in my bank account, too," was his sarcastic response to my words.

Still, he was a real solace to me during that first nightmare week in Walton. "C'mon, soft lad. You've just got to deal with being in here. You just have to accept it. And don't let them get you down," was his advice to me, time and time again. Ian was someone to talk to throughout those long hours in the cell, someone to listen to and someone to have some banter with. Someone, through all this chatting, who was able to allow me to forget, for a while at least, what had happened to me. He was a vital connection for me when every important connection I had had been ripped from me.

I listened to many an interesting story told by Ian about his life dealing with drugs and the like in Liverpool over the years. Oddly enough, his dad had also been involved in this trade and quite obviously had proved himself to be cannier than his own son as he became one of the kingpins of the local drugs world and had managed to avoid being sent to prison himself. The police weren't able to lay a glove on him apparently and he enjoyed the life of Riley in a posh house in Southport.

Hearing some of these stories was a real eye-opener for me. It was all such a different world to my quiet existence in Gaerwen on Ynys Môn and made me realise yet again that I had been transported to a much more chaotic and darker world in here. But as I said earlier, Ian was very streetwise and able to let me in on many a secret about negotiating prison life and how to come through the whole experience.

Although I only spent a week in Walton, as it turned out, I learnt quite a bit about the realities of life in a large prison. I remember walking by a large room on the bottom floor once and seeing a huge batch of what looked like some medicinal product on the tables in this room.

I asked someone what was going on in there. And the answer, like a shot, was delivered in a way that suggested I was quite the innocent in asking such an obvious question. "That's the methadone centre, mate!" came the response. There, quite literally hundreds of inmates would receive treatment for drug addictions. It was both a prison and a drugs centre in a way. The link between drug-taking and life inside became clearer to me every single day.

You could see worse things inside as well. Much, much worse. Once, I witnessed a huge fight going on by one of the pool tables, used during the free hour available for inmates. I was on the landing, watching all of this going on beneath me, as two gangs literally tore into each other, with one poor guy being walloped time and time again with a pool cue. I still remember the frightening noise of that mass fight and seeing blood all over the place. The two gangs were separated fairly quickly by the prison officers, but the one guy who had been hit the most was in was in a hell of a state. I don't know how he could have survived such a beating, but I didn't hear anything about him either way after the experience.

It was a horrifying experience to see such a thing happening in front of your very eyes and brought it home to me again that I was in a very violent place, surrounded by very violent people. A place where such violence could break out at any moment. This fear was with me every single minute I spent in Walton. Who would be the next to be beaten up? Would I be the next victim?

But above the constant fear and worry I felt, the worst part of that week for me was not hearing a single word from my family. Even though I didn't know at the time that they had no idea where I was, I accepted the fact that no connection would be possible with the family at the start.

Ian, the old lag, had told me straight that this lack of family connection at the start was intentional. The prison authorities wanted the inmates to realise that they were now in a totally different space – a totally alien space. "It's all about making sure you know your place now, mate," he told me on more than one occasion. "It's about breaking you – but if you know that, it helps in a way since you feel that you are wise to all their games."

The first Welsh language letter I sent home from Walton was refused by the prison authorities since they didn't have anyone who could translate it for them apparently. It was a scandalous state of affairs, which prevented me from communicating with my family in our mother tongue. Although I was hopping mad about this, what could I do about it? It just seemed to be another way of punishing me and to show that I counted for nothing in their system.

Remember, my spirits were so very low at this time and I did not have any energy to fight against it either. Thankfully, the problem resolved itself after a few days and I was informed that my Welsh-language letter could be sent to my family after all.

In the hopeless situation that I found myself in, I did have one blessing I could turn to. My faith. Faith has always been an important part of my life, ever since my early upbringing in the Wesleyan chapel at Malltraeth during my childhood. And although I later turned away from the chapel to join the church in Wales, it's still the same God that we worship and who watches over us. With everything stacked up against me in such a way in Walton, it was such a daily relief for me to be able to turn to the Most High in prayer every night and simply trust in him that things would improve for me. Despite everything, I had to keep believing that the truth about what had happened would emerge into the light one day.

It's striking how a man's past can come to sustain him and I'll never forget how that trusty old verse came back into my mind in the midst of all the darkness: 'If God is for us, who can be against us?' And perhaps one of these prayers was answered, since on my last day but one at Walton, I was given a job to collect some rubbish bins on the prison site. It was, quite literally, a rubbish job, but at least it was a job and gave me something to do instead of spending all those long and brooding hours torturing myself in that grotty little cell.

In taking this job, I didn't realise I was breaking one of the important protocols among the inmates at Walton. That is, not to assist the system in any way as a prisoner. This was something that many of them took very seriously. Very seriously. I'll never forget walking along the landing to start on my new job and some of the other inmates were standing and scowling at me. Obviously, they had heard there was a 'traitor' in their midst. One of them actually threw some shit at me as I passed by. It was an incredibly unpleasant experience – one of the very worst during my time in jail. It reminded me about that poor prisoner who had been beaten to a pulp with that pool cue. *What the hell have I done in taking this job?* I asked myself. *Am I even going to come out of this place alive?* Everything about this prison was gruesome, but this took things to a new low.

Fortunately, the very same evening, I was told that I was to be moved from Walton and transferred to Kirkham, near Preston. Another prison, yes, but apparently it was much better than this hellhole in Walton. More importantly, there would also be an opportunity to see my family there as well. Finally, things were starting to change for me after an awful run of events that had ruined my life over the last year. Surely Kirkham would be better than this hellhole?

Sian

As you can imagine, there was huge amount of excitement as we prepared to see Dad in prison for the first time. After the first letter arrived here and we filled out the visiting form, it was arranged that we could go and see Dad three weeks exactly after he was sentenced to nine months in jail. We were going to Kirkham, since we had been told that he had been transferred there from Walton.

Social media was just in its early days at this time, but I was able to go on the internet to research the visit. It was such a relief to understand that Kirkham was an 'open prison', where the inmates had more freedom than your usual prison. I also read that Kirkham was linked to a local further education college who had a role in the running of the prison, so that gave me a lot of hope as well. We had, by that point, also received a letter or two from Dad; these were quite brief each time, but at least it made us feel better that things were moving on for him and he was able to do some new things there as well.

The days dragged by as we prepared for the visit. Each day felt like it lasted forever and the time wasn't passing quickly enough. I just wanted to hold Dad tight and tell him that everything would turn out fine. The father-and-daughter relationship is always a very special one in all families, of course, but I've always had an exceptionally close relationship with Dad. I had been through some trauma in my personal life and he had been like a rock for me during all of that. That father-daughter relationship had been taken to a whole new level because of what I went through and all of his support. Now, it was Dad going through his own trials and tribulations. I missed him so terribly during this time. Not having him around was like a deep, physical ache – and an emotional ache, too, with not knowing what was going on with him in Walton.

It was a dark and gloomy November morning when we started on our journey to Kirkham. Me, Arfon and Mam. All of us were just a complete bag of nerves, especially Mam. We had to give her some diazepam – prescribed by her doctor – to calm her nerves before we started out. To be honest, we could all have done with some of that on this particular morning.

After we finally arrived at Kirkham, we had to have a full body search, before we were taken through a maze of corridors to the section of the jail where we were to meet Dad. After reaching this section, we had to go through a series of doors, with each one shutting behind us with a heavy thud every time. Each thud reminded us that we were in a place where people were locked up and shut away from the world. Away from society. Away from people. Away from their families.

We were then led to a large room in the furthest part of the prison and the three of us were asked to sit down by a table and wait. For an hour and a half. My stomach was churning, my mouth was like a camel's armpit and my hands were shaking uncontrollably. I don't know how I managed to hold back the tears. I was in such a state.

Seeing Dad walking into the room three weeks after we last saw him in the court in Caernarfon was such an emotional experience for all three of us. My first impression was that Dad had lost weight and that he had a very pained expression on his face. He was wearing an orange hi-vis, along with old blue jeans and a blue-and-white shirt – the uniform all inmates were expected to wear at Kirkham. This struck me as completely bizarre. Dad in jeans? I'd never seen him wearing jeans in my whole life. Somehow, that seemed to sum it all up. A clear sign how things had been upended for Dad – and our lives, too.

"What on earth are you wearing Dad?" I asked him in amazement.

"My new uniform," he said, quietly. The old humour was still there despite everything.

The long and close group hug that followed showed that nothing had changed in the strong bond between us as a family. We then had to be separated, with Dad having to sit in a chair away from the table and the three of us sitting around the table.

Dad then launched into a series of questions about the family and how his grandchildren were getting on – Jade, Arthur Huw and Mared. That was so Dad, wanting to ask about the family. It was also a way of avoiding having to talk very much about his own experiences in prison.

"But how are you, Dad?" I asked, interrupting him several times. "That's the important question today."

"Oh, I'm okay, Sian," he said, but his eyes told me very clearly that he wasn't okay at all.

"At least this place is a bit better than that hellhole in Walton," he added with a sigh.

We tried to get him to say some more about Walton then, but it was clear that he didn't want to share much with us – wanting to protect us from the harsh realities, no doubt. As good as he is at mixing with other people, Dad is a very private individual at heart and that hasn't changed at all over the years. Even today, I don't think we have heard the full story of his week in Walton Prison from him. There are some things he's holding back from us as a family – things he wants to keep to himself. Keeping these in his own mind. Keeping them safe in there. As hard as that is for us as a family, we just have to respect his wishes.

We only had an hour with Dad that morning, the time flying by so quickly.

Almost before we really got going, a prison officer announced, sharply, "Time's up!" and that was it, the visit was over.

We had to leave Dad behind in his strange prison uniform, looking forlornly at us as we left the visiting room. Having to say goodbye that morning was even harder than the morning in Caernarfon Crown Court in a way. We had had Dad back for an hour, but now he was being taken away from us again... and so much had been left unsaid!

I remember leaving Kirkham in a very tearful state and feeling very frustrated as well. I hadn't had the answers to all those questions that had been swirling around in my head for so long. And then we had to face the long drive back to Wales – in complete silence. All three of us, in our own way, were trying to process what we had just experienced in the jail and were trying to hold on – for dear life – to every single world Dad had said during that hour, which wasn't a lot, to be honest. However, we had to squeeze everything we could out of those precious words and hold on to them in our own individual minds. It would be another few weeks before we could see Dad again in Kirkham.

Noel

It was so good to see Eira, Sian and Arfon that day in Kirkham. A very emotional day for the four of us, obviously, but it was so good to revisit that family connection that has always been so important to us all. For me, it was good to have an update on how every member of the family was getting on – and a way for me to deflect all the questions about how I was. I didn't want to burden the family with all that. I just wasn't sure how I was going to be honest and I didn't want to go there. So, it was much easier for me to be firing the questions and asking how everybody was.

Questions aside, it was such a huge relief for me to know that my family were one hundred per cent behind me. After all the questions I had been asking *myself* over the past three weeks under lock and key, knowing that was so, so reassuring and so uplifting.

It was also good to be able to share with them that quite a few letters were now reaching me in Kirkham, something that would continue right up to the time I was released from prison, three months down the line. These were letters from my fellow councillors on Ynys Môn Council, such as Goronwy Parry, Gwyn Jones, Gwilym O Jones and Bessie Burns. Along with letters from politicians such as Albert Owen, the Labour MP for Ynys Môn at the time, and Eurig Wyn, who was a Member of the European Parliament for Plaid Cymru. Knowing that individuals of such quality were thinking of me and still believing in me, despite everything, was a huge boost, I can tell you.

One other thing that raised my spirits no end was receiving the football scores every week from Aled Jones, Malltraeth – an old family friend of ours. Aled collected these all together for me on a Saturday afternoon and posted them that evening, so that I would receive them either on a Monday or a Tuesday. I can't tell you how happy that made me feel. It gave me a feeling that some normality was coming back into my life again, as following the football scores every Saturday had been such a key part of my life for so many years. A very simple thing, I know, but it meant the world to me. I'll always be indebted to Aled for that kind weekly gesture all the time I was in Kirkham.

The moment I arrived at Kirkham after a week at Walton, things seemed to pick up for me. Kirkham was an old RAF camp, a huge site on the outskirts of Preston, but from the very start there was something more open about the place. To start off with, I wasn't locked up for twenty-three hours a day in my cell and I also had my own cell in a billet that included some twenty people. Secondly, the whole purpose of Kirkham was to try and prepare the inmates for returning to everyday life in society after their period in the jail. There was a clear emphasis on rehabilitation here and everyone was treated so much better somehow. Thirdly, I was given some work that suited me so much better than the bin collection I had been doing at the end of my stint at Walton. I got this work after attending the induction session that each new inmate had to undergo after reaching Kirkham, where there was an opportunity for us to talk about your experiences and interests etc. I mentioned that I was interested in gardening to the Prison Authorities and I was then located on the large farm they had as a part of the site, which was run by Lancaster College.

This farm took up many acres of the site and included huge greenhouses as well. During my first week, I was planting flowers. I then had to prepare thousands of pots to hold the plants – washing them and getting them in order, before they were then sold. The farm had a very good reputation apparently and had won several awards at the Lancashire Show along the years. With the money gained from this and some other ventures, such as the creation of garden benches and dog kennels, it brought quite a lot of finance into the college.

An old lag who was running the greenhouses took a liking to me for some reason and would often say to me in the morning, "Look after them, Taff, I'll be back at lunchtime." This was a reference to the others there – most of them younger than myself – who I was expected to keep an eye on. Many of these young lads had been sent to prison for speeding offences, which was ridiculous in my opinion. I was able to get along with them quite well, despite the fact that they could be so noisy, as well as their practice of playing their ghetto blasters on full blast at night in their cells and keeping us all awake! This got to be such a problem that some of us, who were slightly older, decided to go and see the Governor of Kirkham to ask whether we could be moved to an empty billet nearby. He was a very reasonable chap and agreed to the move. So, the 'golden oldies' moved to the other billet and got some more peace and quiet in there, thank God.

I got used to the new routine in Kirkham quite quickly. I was still in prison, yes, but at least I was able to work and do something of interest to me as well. It helped my mood tremendously. The work shift began around 8.30am and lasted until 4pm, and I was given around £10 a week for my efforts. This money would be spent in the tuckshop at the camp. Biscuits and chocolate was my usual choice – I've always had a sweet tooth! Then, after supper at night, all of us would go on an evening walk – twice around the whole camp, which was around two miles in all. It was a chance to stretch our legs and have a chat among ourselves before retiring for the evening.

As it happens, Ynys Môn – the island connection again – raised an interesting point for me when I was changing the laundry one week. A guy in there said he had a caravan at Trearddur Bay and after asking about my experiences and why I was in prison, he said, "I've heard that quite a few of you have been caught up in all this business, you know."

This was very encouraging news for me. All along this process, the Post Office had insisted that I was the only one to be caught out in this way. They repeated this time and time again. No problem anywhere else, they said. But the words of Mr Caravan Man in Kirkham suggested to me that there was more to this story and led me to start asking whether other people had been put through the wringer just as I had been.

To be honest, finding such hope was like coming across some unexpected treasure in Kirkham. There was a very long and complicated treasure hunt ahead of me in the years to come, but I felt that the first clue had been revealed to me in that conversation.

* * *

Prison Letters

7.11.06
Number W46196
HMP Liverpool
6 Hornby Road
Walton
Liverpool

Dear Eira and family
I have let everyone down. No fault on anyone but myself. But, I'm extremely disappointed with that verdict. It's a hell of a shock to find myself in such a place as this.

Having said that, I am sharing with a lad from Birkenhead called Ian. I am going to one or two courses to learn about computers... ha ha!

Please say hello to everyone, especially Jade, Mared and Arthur Huw.

Also, I need clothes and slippers, trainers, bathroom items, cod liver oil tablets and Vitamin C.

Regards to you all.
Much love
Noel

PS I'm trying to get a pass for you to come and see me - only three at once.

* * *

13.11.06
HMP Kirkham
Kirkham
Lancashire

Dear Eira

Good news. I have moved to J Wing 21, also I have had a job outdoors cleaning and gardening work. Also, I won't be locked up so much here, just at night.

I must say I miss everyone so much. Be strong and hold your head up high. I haven't killed anyone but I have hurt everyone else. I have asked to see the Citizens Advice in a week. Post is in my head and I have to try and sort it or I will be in here for a longer spell.

They are up in arms here as Liverpool and Everton have lost again. I don't see a paper until it's about three days later – no Sky or TV in here.

An awful Christmas ahead of me. Missing my 60th birthday and missing the children opening their presents.

Much Love
Noel.

***

17.11.06
HMP Kirkham
Kirkham
Lancashire

Dear Eira

Thank you for the letter. It was so good to be able to speak on the phone. I have met the son of Alun Williams, the Solicitor and he has helped me a lot.

Yes, I'm still feeling low here, but it's a lot better in here than Liverpool.

I'm hoping to get a job in the Garden on Friday.

I'm looking forward to see you on Friday – I miss you all so much.
Much Love
Noel.

* * *

13.11.06

Dear Eira

Well, it's nearly December 1st and we are counting the weeks here.

I've been in the clinic today checking my blood pressure and I need to go back there next week.

I'm hoping to move to a billet for those aged over 40. Unfortunately, the young lads in here make a terrible racket at times, with loud music playing until late. Looking forward to see my fancy ladies tomorrow, and Arfon!

I have asked for more visiting orders by next month.

Letters are still arriving and I am thankful for them.

I've got to go for supper now. I so miss your home cooking.

Much love to you all.

Noel Xxx

* * *

Dear Eira, Arfon and Sian

Well, that's Christmas over and done with thank God.

Just the new year left now. Counting the days after that. I hope Jade, Arthur and Mared were pleased by what they got from Santa.

Best Regards

Noel xxx

* * *

12.11.06

Dear All

Boredom is the worst part and I get very emotional when I receive so many letters of support. The nights are so very long. I miss everyone terribly and the children.

Much Love, Noel.

Apologies for creating all this bother.

* * *

24.11.06

Dear All

Huge panic here on Friday evening – one of the lads managed to escape but he has been caught by now. I've been to church listening to a crew of gospel singers. They were very good.

I have found a place at the Education centre on Monday. What I'm going to do God only knows. A poor night's sleep last night. I'm going to go back to the doctor.

* * *

12.12.06

Dear All

I have had a lot of cards and letters again, every day nearly. The weather is wild here, wind and rain every day. Don't send me anything for Christmas. It's not worth it. I will be home before long after that hopefully.

We've had the Christmas Menu – it looks good.

Breakfast: Bacon or Cornflakes

Lunch: Turkey, Sprouts, Carrots and Xmas Pud

Tea: Gammon, Pork Pie, Drink

Supper: Mince Pie or Christmas Cake

***

December 2006.

Letter from the former European MSP Eurig Wyn, Waunfawr

Here is a note I should have written a while back, but better late than never.

I hope you are feeling more yourself by now following all your troubles.

I'm sure you will be happy to know that all your contemporaries think the world of you – and fully appreciate the principled person that you are. The testimony of your community conveys all that clearly.

Say hello to all members of the family. We will have an opportunity to catch up when the time comes again to promote Plaid's cause.

My very best wishes.

Eurig.

CHAPTER 6

Coming Back Home

My time in Kirkham was rushing by and I was finding myself adapting to a life under lock and key. The work was keeping me busy and occupied, and I had to come to know the gang who were in with me quite well, too. Apart from one quite unpleasant guy from Blackpool, who was in for several serious offences, you could say that the rest were just petty criminals, who shouldn't have been sent to jail at all in the first place.

It was a waste of money and a complete waste of time, in my opinion. And there was the even worse danger of these young lads becoming institutionalised and developing a habit of being in jail, which would be very hard to shake off in life. I was starting to see that the so-called 'justice system' was so wrong in so many ways. But apart from all that, there was a lot of leg-pulling going on between all of us, with everybody trying to make the best of it and sustain each other's spirits; putting our heads down and waiting for our time inside to come to an end.

It was a different world altogether to Walton. All the constant fear and anxiety I had experienced in Walton 24/7 had disappeared. Yes, of course, there was still frustration at what had happened to me, but that sensation was easier for me to live with, for sure. However, during this time at Kirkham, when I was just starting to find my feet in a way, one big disappointment came my way – even though I was half-expecting it, if truth be told.

A letter arrived for me from Meirion Jones, who was the Ynys Môn Council's solicitor, informing me that after the court decision, the council had to dismiss me as a councillor. I don't blame Meirion or the county council since they were only following the letter of the law in doing so. Having said that, from what I understand, had I been given a sentence of six months rather than nine months, I could have kept my place on the county council. It was a big blow when that news came through.

Being a county councillor for Gaerwen had been such an important part of my life for so many years – over fifteen years, all in all – and the council work was very close to my heart. I was in no way one of the leading lights on the county council, but yet again I felt I was making a contribution there and helping the people of Gaerwen for being so kind as to vote me in as their local representative. And now all this was being ripped away from me. I knew that a letter of this type was likely to come my way, but there was something so final in what was said. There was no way back for me now as a county councillor. Having reached a state of acceptance of my lot at Kirkham, receiving this letter was a huge setback, there's no doubt about it.

I spent the next few days in another deep depression, with all the unfairness of the case coming over me in waves again. I had lost my freedom, I had lost my good name, I had lost my job and now I had lost the community role that was so important for me in Gaerwen. Losing seemed to have become a way of life for me. Luckily, for me, there was support from other directions, which I had to hold on to for dear life. The letters of support from back home were still coming in and people also came to visit me at Kirkham quite regularly.

The family visited like clockwork, of course, and some other friends also made the long journey to Kirkham. One good friend and a fellow councillor, Trefor Lloyd Hughes from Holyhead, made the journey twice. I'm very thankful to him for standing by me. Seeing Trefor and his warm words of support went a good way to making up for the bitter blow of losing my role as a county councillor. And all this led to even better news for me.

After being at Kirkham for three months, I was summoned by the governor to his office where he told me I was to be released in a few days' time. What a feeling of relief to hear such news and to be able to think about going home to my family and my community at last. I've got to say, though, there was some nervousness as well. What kind of reception would I get when I came home? What on earth would I do with myself, having lost not one, but two jobs? How would I even begin to prove to people that I was innocent of the charge that sent me to prison?

All these questions were whizzing around in my head in the days leading up to the release date. I just knew in my heart of hearts that I would have another mountain to climb after going home – but perhaps I hadn't fully understood how steep that mountain would be...

Sian

The day when we were told of Dad's release from Kirkham was a day of huge celebration in our home. We hadn't had an idea of how much of the nine months Dad would have to serve, even though we were hopeful he could be released about halfway through the sentence. Knowing what we did about Dad and his good character, we were sure that 'good behaviour' would count in his favour in this respect – and so it proved.

At last – after three months, which had been such a nightmare for us as a family – Dad was coming home! Mam, Edwin, Gel, Arfon, Auntie Gwenda and myself were in seventh heaven thinking about getting him back with us and for the family to be complete once again. And not to have to take that long journey to Preston and back again, thank God!

It was decided that it would be me and Arfon who would make that last journey to collect Dad on his release day. As Dad was being released first thing in the morning, we had decided to go up the day before and stay the night in a hotel near Preston.

After arriving at the hotel, Arfon and I went down for a drink in the bar that evening and someone standing at the bar asked us what we were doing in the area: "Oh, we're just going up to Scotland for a few days," I said immediately, almost without thinking. I did not want to admit that we were actually there to collect our dad from prison.

"Oh, you'll really enjoy yourselves," he replied. "It's lovely up there!"

I just smiled back to him, praying he wouldn't ask any more questions. Looking back, I feel guilty about not being honest on this occasion. But at the time, it didn't make any sense at all to me that Dad was in prison and having to acknowledge that to a stranger would be even more nonsensical. It was just too much to ask.

I can't begin to tell you what it felt like to see him walking out of Kirkham Prison that day, in his own clothes this time –not that terrible uniform he had to wear every time we saw him there previously. He was carrying a huge bag with him, which not only had his personal items, but all the cards and letters he had received from people during his time within.

"How do you feel Dad bach?" I asked him at the gates of the prison, while giving him a long, warm hug.

"As if I'm returning from hell," he said, with a huge sigh of relief.

That said it all, to be honest – from his perspective and from ours as a family as well. We then jumped in the car to drive back to north Wales and back to his roots, to Malltraeth. We had arranged for Mam and Dad to come and stay with me for a while until we got our lives back on track. As it happened, Mam and Dad would stay with me for a whole year before moving back to Gaerwen itself.

I was so glad that Dad was able to be back where he was born and brought up during that year, among people he knew so well and in an area that was so close to his heart as well. This was very important because the year ahead was going to be a very difficult and challenging twelve months for us all, financially and practically, as we had to face the cold reality of life *after* prison – the extent of which we couldn't really have anticipated beforehand.

However, in the sheer joy and excitement that day driving back from Kirkham, we simply had no idea what exactly was ahead of us and what the fallout would be for each one of us. Dad had been released, but there were a good few chains around him still – and some of those were literal chains as it turned out.

Noel

One of the conditions of being released early from Kirkham was to have to wear a tag on my ankle for three months. I never thought for a moment what a curse this bloody tag would prove to be after leaving prison. Having to wear it 24/7 was worse than being in jail itself – and that's the honest truth.

A firm came to place the tag on my ankle the very evening I came home to Malltraeth. I wasn't even allowed to have my first night of freedom without being incarcerated again. The tag sent a signal to a company based in Pwllheli to show where I was all the time, day and night. Talk about Big Brother! One of the conditions imposed with wearing the tag was that I *had* to be back in the house by 7pm each evening. If I happened to arrive home a minute after 7pm, I would immediately be sent back to jail. As you can imagine, this created a huge amount of stress for me and it was constantly playing on my mind, wherever I was and whatever I was doing every day. I was constantly having nightmares about being stuck somewhere and not being able to reach home by 7pm. I was living on my nerves every day, dreading not being able to make the deadline.

Funnily enough, a seasoned jailbird at Kirkham had shown me how to take off the tag.

Noel with his first bike at 7 years of age

Noel with his parents at Maltraeth

Noel with Antie Madge from America

Noel and Eira with their parents

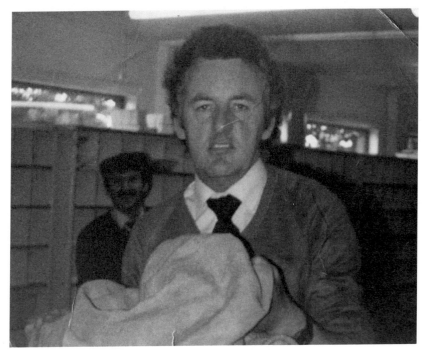

At work as a postman

Noel with Joan and Non, his American cousins

Noel, Eira, Arfon, Edwin and Sian

Sian with her brothers Edwin and Arfon

Noel at an Ynys Mon council function

Another family gathering

A Thomas family gathering

At a Post Office awards ceremony

Noel with his cousins Alan, Medwyn, Gordon and Joan

Noel with his soilicitor Neil Hudgell

Noel with his work colleagues in the Post Office in Llangefni

Noel and his wife Eira in the Post Office at Gaerwen

Family memories with Jade, Kaden and Eira

Noel in his sanctuary at Eglwys Tal Llyn

Noel with Lorraine Williams, another local Sub Postmaster who was prosecuted by the Post Office

With Neil Hudgell and barrister Tim Maloney ahead of the Appeal Court Hearing in April 2021

Noel with fellow Sub Postmaster Jo Hamilton

With fellow Sub Postmaster Lee Castleton outside Court of Appeal

Noel with the other jubilant Sub Postmasters outside the HighCourt in 2019

Noel being interviewed by journalist Nick Wallis

The family at the ceremony held by Ynys Mon County Council

Sian Thomas, Noel Thomas and Aled Gwyn Job

At Eglwys Tal Llyn

With Eleanor Shaikh

"Look, Taff," he told me. "It's bloody easy. You can take it off like this and they'll have no clue about it. You'll be able to laugh at their stupid little system!"

He was only trying to be helpful and wanting me to 'give it to the man', so to speak, but I wasn't willing to take the risk as I couldn't bear the idea of going back to jail and I couldn't put the family through that again either. For the sake of all of us, I had to keep to the rules.

Wearing the tag was horrible, to tell you the truth. I felt as if I was a sheep who had been branded by a local farmer. The tag reminded me that I still belonged to the jail system and that I was still their possession even though I was officially a free man. There was just no escaping this day-and-night monitoring.

But we had a big problem with this from the off. You see, Sian's house in Malltraeth was in a bit of a dip and, as such, the signal was not being picked up all the time. I lost count of how many times officers turned up at the door in Malltraeth, insisting on knowing where I was, as the signal had been lost. At other times, the phone would ring constantly at night, checking up on me. I'll never forget the security team barging into mine and Eira's bedroom one evening while we were sleeping and insisting they had to see the tag. "Take the duvet off now!" one of them ordered. "We've got to check you're still wearing the tag!" It was one of the most humiliating experiences that came my way throughout the whole saga. It was a form of psychological torture looking back at it all now. I might have left jail, but it was as if the authorities wanted to remind me constantly that I was still imprisoned and under their rules – at their beck and call, night and day.

I have always been a walker, but after returning to Malltraeth, walking became even more important in my life. I'm sure that this burning desire to walk for miles each day was my body's natural response to the feeling of still being in prison because of the blasted tag. But it was also a way for me to clear my mind and release stress. I took daily walks to some nearby beauty spots at Llanddwyn,

Niwbwrch, Aberffraw and Dothan, and would quite literally go for hours and hours every day.

Tal-y-Llyn church near Aberffraw became almost a place of pilgrimage for me. There's no doubt that this became my favourite place of all during this period of adjusting to life after prison. The fact that the church itself is out of the way – and almost a mile away from the nearest farm – made it even more special in my view. Being able to go there and sit in silence for about fifteen to thirty minutes at a time was probably one of the main things that kept me sane during this difficult time. I just felt there was a quiet presence there that guarded over me, despite everything that was happening to me. Even to this day, I just love going to this little church by myself or with a member of the family. Every time I step over its threshold, I always remember the peace of mind this church gave me during the most difficult time of my life and I give silent thanks for that provision to the most high every time as well.

Sian

None of us had thought for a moment that this blooming tag would prove to be such a problem once Dad came home. But it proved to be constant pain for all of us. I decided to keep the phone on top of an old wardrobe in my bedroom to try and spare Mam and Dad from the hassle of people phoning the house all the time. But being able to sleep proved to be almost impossible, since it was nothing for the tag team to phone four, five times a night to check up on Dad. It soon became a complete farce.

They would phone and ask; "Where's your father? Can we talk to him, please?" And I would then have to say he was sleeping next door and have to go to wake him up just for him to confirm he was at home. Dad would say, "Yes, I'm here," and give his name and date of birth to them in a sleepy-dazed state. Before long, I came to know the people who were phoning. But going through the motions with them for three whole months was just ridiculous.

All this rigmarole played havoc with my sleep and the sleep

of my parents for the whole three months that Dad had to wear the tag. Even today, my sleep pattern is still not as it should be and there's no doubt in my mind that this three-month nightmare was a big part of that. It was just so unfair and oppressive that this tag team were phoning every hour or so, and even though they said it was the lack of signal that caused them to phone so regularly, I don't doubt it was the prison system that insisted on it – as if we hadn't suffered enough as it was.

One of the other things I found to be so frustrating at this time was that Dad didn't let us know how he was really feeling. A typical man, perhaps, but typical Dad as well. So private. So much of a wall at times. "How are you feeling today, Dad?" I would ask him all the time. "Oh, I'm alright, Sian," was the stock response each time. This was his signal that he didn't want to talk about how he was feeling. I didn't have a clue about what was going through his mind. He couldn't share things with his own daughter, even though we had always been so close. This broke my heart.

He was quite obviously depressed since he was not allowed to do the work he loved so much nor was he able to be a councillor either, which had given him so much of a sense of purpose in life. He seemed completely lost and adrift at this time. A vulnerable man. A broken man.

Every day, he would disappear for hours on his walks and we would quite often have *no* idea where he was during these hours of walking. I remember Edwin and I in a blind panic one day when he hadn't returned home after several hours of walking. We went out to look for him – me in one car and Edwin in another car. We searched and searched for him throughout the area, with no sight of him anywhere. The two of us were scared stiff and had to return home to think what we could do next. And who did we see sitting on the front wall outside the house? Dad.

"Where the hell have you been, Dad?" I asked to him in my temper and my worry. "The two of us have been out looking for you for hours, worried sick about you!"

"Just out walking," he responded, quite coolly.

As relieved as I was to see him safe, I could have throttled him after causing such panic and distress for me and Edwin. That was one scary day, I can tell you, but I think that some good came from this event as well. Dad seemed to sense the panic he had caused and came to see that he needed to respond in some way and communicate in a new way with us. Perhaps things could change, after all.

Noel

How did I feel in this period after coming home? Well, to be honest, that initial feeling of euphoria after being released from jail wore off very quickly. As I mentioned earlier, it was as if I was still in jail in a way because of the tag I had to wear all the time. And on top of all that, I had to live in my daughter's home because of what had happened. The shame weighed very heavily on my mind.

There was a huge lack of purpose in my life. I was not able to do the job that had meant so much to me for twelve years in the Post at Gaerwen. Waking up to this realisation every morning was a complete nightmare. A dreadful empty feeling came over me every single day and refused to budge. In addition, I had lost the role of county councillor, representing my community in Gaerwen. This hurt just as badly, if not worse, and I came to realise what an essential part of my life being a councillor had been for me. Talking to people, listening to their viewpoints and trying to help them the best I could. Being their representative and trying to convey their voice within the county council had been so, so important for me. It was as if the Noel Thomas I knew, and other people knew, had ceased to be somehow.

And if all this was not enough, there was no money coming in at all. I was sixty years old and on the scrapheap. The humiliation was complete when I had to declare myself bankrupt. It was the only option for me, unfortunately. The prospects of getting a new job at my age seemed to be remote, if not downright impossible. You can well imagine how I was feeling in view of all this.

After a while, I decided I had to look for help – for my own sake and for my family's sake.

Something had to change. Thanks to Dr Ben and Dr Bethan in the family surgery in Star, a number of counselling sessions were arranged for me with a counsellor in Caernarfon. I had around twelve sessions in all, from what I can remember. To this day, I'm very grateful for the help I received from the counsellor – a lovely woman from Caernarfon itself.

It may sound odd for me to say this, but it was easier for me to pour out my heart to a stranger than to do that with my close family. I remember feeling guilty about this, with us being such a close family in so many other ways, but I'll never forget the counsellor telling me: "Noel, you don't have to feel guilty about this at all. You would be amazed how many people say that to me at the start. That's the whole point of counselling – being able to open your heart to someone outside the close family circle and someone who can look at things from a whole new perspective." Hearing this was very encouraging. It gave me permission, in a way, to reveal things I hadn't been brave enough to tell my family. The female counsellor was brilliant in just listening patiently to me go through everything and then being able to offer a few other alternatives for me to consider and new ways to think about my situation.

We discussed the lot over the next few weeks. The shame, the anger, the guilt, the dark thoughts and feelings, the frustration, and all the fears and anxieties I had about things in general. I've got to say that these sharing session were proving to be very cathartic for me. And for someone who's not the best at sharing how I feel, this all came as a big surprise. At the end of the twelve sessions, I felt as if a huge weight had been lifted off my shoulders. I'll be forever grateful to the counsellor for all her help. I don't know how things would have panned out for me without her help. That's the honest truth.

Of course, nothing had changed in my circumstances on the outside. There were huge problems I had to face and there seemed to be no shifting on these, but at least this counsellor had offered me a glimmer of light that there could be a way ahead for me after all.

Sian

As wonderful as it was to have Dad back home with us, this was the start of a whole new period of different problems. One huge headache was the Proceeds of Crime Act used by the Royal Mail to insist that Dad had to pay back monies for his 'crime' and pay their legal costs as well, which must have been quite high in view of the battalion of solicitors they had turning up for duty every time Dad was in court.

In the first place, we had to pay back a portion of the £52,000 that Dad had 'stolen' from the Post Office and this sum had to be paid back immediately. This came to £10,000 – but, quite simply, we didn't have that sort of money available. I decided that I would have to sell my home in Malltraeth so that we could pay this money, but Dad was dead against this to start with.

"It's my problem," he would say, regularly. "I'm the one who should find a way to settle it, Sian. It's just not fair that you have to sell your own home to help me."

And my answer: "Look, Dad, you have to accept help from your family. What's the point of family if they can't help you at a time like this?"

After digging in his heels for a while, Dad had to swallow his pride and accept that my idea made sense for us all as a family. In losing what was by then their home in Malltraeth, Dad and Mam could make an application to have a house for rent back in Gaerwen – and that's exactly what happened about a year down the line. They were given a pensioners' bungalow in the Rhos Ellen council estate in the middle of the village.

It was by no means an easy decision to make, though. I had been living alone in my home at Malltraeth for over ten years and I was very happy there as well. However, I had to help Mam and Dad out of this deep hole in which they had found themselves through no fault of their own. I had part-bought my home in Malltraeth with a local housing association, Cymdeithas Tai Eryri, and, luckily for me, I was able to sell the house within a matter of weeks after informing them of my decision. The profits from the sale could then go towards paying off the debt to the Royal Mail.

This in itself was not going to be enough to clear all the costs, so Dad received legal advice to sell the family home that adjoined the Post Office in Gaerwen. Once again, the family was able to pull together to help Mam and Dad sell the house to my brother, Edwin, and his wife, Gail. This was a battle, too, with the Royal Mail arguing for three years that there was a charge on the house and insisting that Edwin would have to pay for this charge. He held his ground, thankfully, and in the end, the Royal Mail dropped the charge. It was a huge relief for us all.

The years between 2006 and 2009 were very tough for us as a family – very tough financially with having to pay off the £10,000 mentioned earlier, but tough as well as we tried desperately to find a new role for Dad, a new purpose for him in life. He was in his sixties and everything he had ever worked for in his life had been taken away from him. He was a broken man after his experiences in prison, a shadow of who he used to be, and he seemed to have lost all hope of being able to prove his innocence one day.

Since Dad had 'given up the ghost', it meant someone had to step up within the family. And for some reason, this task fell on my shoulders. I've always been quite a determined individual and someone who hates injustice, so in a way it was natural that I should be the one to do the work. I was adamant that we would clear Dad's name one way or the other, even though I hadn't the slightest idea how we would be able to do that. I had no experience. No contacts. No legal background. No idea, really. Just a heart for Dad. And a heart for the truth, as well.

I decided to start some research on the internet. Back then, of course, social media hadn't come into its own, so there was not that much information available for your average citizen to search online. Even so, I started down the information road – and what a long and winding road that would prove to be.

Noel

The financial pressures on myself and the family was just unbearable during those early years after coming home from jail. The saga of selling Sian's house first, then the saga of Edwin buying the Old Post was so very stressful all round. On top of this, the Royal Mail wanted to take away my pension as an additional cost for what had happened. Understand this: they wanted to take forty-two years' worth of contributions from me. They wanted to delete forty-two years of my life, in essence. It was just stress upon stress upon stress at this time.

If there was any doubt about how cold and heartless this organisation was – the employer I had given forty-two years of service to – this was the ultimate proof. The punishment, the beating… the torture just went on and on and there was no sign that it was coming to an end either. It almost seemed to me that they took some perverse pleasure in kicking a man when he was down. With no sort of salary coming in at all, the thought of losing my pension on top of all that was just more salt on the wound. How on earth was I to live at all?

My spirits were at an all-time low. It was much worse than the time in prison even. It was so difficult for poor Eira to cope with this from day to day, and just as difficult for everyone else in the family as well. It was if I had gone from prison hell to a living hell. Yes, we had been able to come back to live in Gaerwen and we had been fortunate to be given a council bungalow in the centre of the village, but there were all these other shadows hanging over me 24/7. It was as if the court sentence in Caernarfon that day still stood and I was still in a state of constant imprisonment.

Thank God a ray of light appeared on the horizon at last, after I was able to arrange a meeting with the judge (and soccer commentator) Nic Parry in Mold, as part of a meeting with the Royal Mail on the matter.

"How long have you been working for them, Noel?" he asked me during the meeting.

"Forty-two years," I replied.

"Right. Leave it with me. I will sort this out for you," he said in a very decisive way.

And thankfully, Nic Parry managed to ensure that they were not able to get their hands on my pension. Right in the middle of a very dark and hopeless time, this came as a lifeline for a drowning man. I'm very indebted to Nic Parry for what he managed to do for me that day.

Despite all the darkness around me, I hadn't given up on my faith and God hadn't let go of me either. And although one or two people had made things difficult for me on my return to church every Sunday at Gaerwen, the majority of the worshippers were very glad to see me there and made me feel right at home again.

As it happens, at exactly the same time as I went back to live in Gaerwen, a new vicar came to serve in the village, called Emlyn Cadwaladr Williams. Emlyn comes from a nearby village on the island, Pentraeth, and from the very start he proved to be very supportive. There's a real strength to Emlyn's personality and he has his feet planted firmly on the ground as well. His ministry has been a blessing to me and the family. I really like Emlyn's style of preaching, too. He stands among us as worshippers rather than going up from the pulpit; he speaks with us, rather than speaking at us in a way. His messages are always short and purposeful, no longer than around ten minutes long and each one including a punchy story, too, which always manages to keep your attention. I'm sure that our churches on Ynys Môn would be in a much more flourishing state if they all followed Emlyn's style of preaching. 'Let those who have ears, listen,' as they say!

Despite this, the weeks, months, years were rushing by and the work situation still appeared to be as hopeless as ever. I had to live on the dole during this time, had to visit the dole office and go through the motions of looking for work. Of course, being in my early sixties, there were not many opportunities at all. To be perfectly honest, though, neither my mind or my heart were in the right place to even think about work during those first three years after coming home from prison.

I can see now how my whole personality had changed for the worse after the experience that came my way. From being a joyful person, who was full of life and who enjoyed every single day, I turned into a joyless, depressive person who saw everything as a huge burden and a huge effort, with no patience at all for those things I used to enjoy doing.

"But you are home now, Noel, with your family and back in your community," some of my friends would tell me regularly.

"Yes, that's true, and thanks be to God for that. But…" was my answer.

People around me didn't quite understand how much of a dark shadow was hanging over me and following me wherever I went every day. Would this shadow ever leave me? This was the real fear that kept me awake so often at night. The idea that I had been branded for life as a criminal and that this would never, ever change. Eira would say that I would wake up regularly in the middle of the night, bathed in sweat, shouting out; "Help! Help!" Nightmares at night and nightmares during the day – this was my life during the period after coming out of jail.

Despite all the wonderful support I received from my family, the counselling, the walking and in settling some of the biggest financial problems, it was hard for me to see that there was any future for me. I was stuck in very deep hole and there were precious few signs that I would be able to climb out of this deep hole. There was nothing at all on the media, either nationally or locally, offering any hope that anything was on the horizon that could change things for me. I can't begin to describe how frustrating and hopeless this was at the time, especially as I knew full well that I hadn't stolen a single penny from my Post Office in Gaerwen. I had begun to believe that I would take this to my grave, without being able to prove it to anyone apart from myself.

The harsh truth was this: how could I prove anything, as all the evidence I had proving my innocence had gone up in flames during the fire in the Post Office in Bangor? And with no mention anywhere else that any other sub-postmaster had been implicated in the same way as I had been, it all seemed completely hopeless. I was all on my own, in a post-prison hell. And it was a terribly lonely place to be, believe you me.

Little did I know then, in the midst of my darkness, that 2008 would change everything for me and my family. And that three events would take place during that year that would give me hope, at last, that there *was* new evidence out there. Evidence that could haul me out of the deep, dark pit I was in.

CHAPTER 7

The Tide Begins to Turn

In this chapter, we will continue to tell the story from Noel and Sian's perspective alternatively, but we will also summarise some of the key legal and political facts that came to light during this period by means of a third voice.

Noel

2008 was a big year. A big year for both myself and my family. You see, this was the year that some light emerged at the end of that long and dark tunnel that I'd been travelling through for three whole years. '*Tri Chynnig i Gymro*,' we say in Welsh ('three opportunities for a Welshman') and this saying certainly came true for me in this year with three events happening in a very short period over a few weeks in May, as if the pieces of the jigsaw were falling into place at last.

The first of these pieces to fall into place was that a local journalist with the BBC, a guy called Sion Tecwyn, called by to see me in my house in Gaerwen. I had come to know Sion fairly well over the years, since he would phone me up quite regularly to find out what was going on with Ynys Môn County Council, especially at the time when things were going pear-shaped there – as I have mentioned earlier. Anyway, on this occasion, it wasn't Ynys Môn Council on his mind, but something that was much more important – news that would start to prise open the door of that cell I was still living in, even though I had been released from prison three years previously – and give me some hope, at last!

Sion Tecwyn had been following a story about the Halal Meat Plant that morning and on his way back to the BBC in Bangor, he called by to see me.

"Noel," he told me at the door, "there's a story going round the newsroom in Bangor about a magazine called *Computer Weekly*."

"What's that then, Sion?" I asked. I had never heard of it.

"It's an IT magazine," he answered. "I haven't looked into it properly, but the talk in the office is that that *Computer Weekly* has found out some things about the Horizon IT company."

And in leaving that morning, his parting shot was: "This could change everything for you, Noel."

Nothing more was said that morning, but hearing this news was a huge boost and I made a mental note to look at *Computer Weekly* on the internet during the next few days.

However, before I had the chance to do that, another piece of the jigsaw arrived – this time in the form of a letter from a gentleman called Roch Garrard from Hampshire. He had taken the trouble to write to me to let me know that a case very similar to mine had happened to his village sub-postmaster in a place called South Warnborough. Roch Garrard was a retired probation officer and part of a group in the village who were trying to support Jo Hamilton, the local sub-postmistress, after she had been placed on probation for 'stealing' money from her local Post Office.

'As villagers,' he wrote, 'we are trying to collect information about similar cases as we believe there's something seriously wrong with the Post Office's computerised system. The newspaper reports we have read suggest you have suffered in the same way as Jo Hamilton – but to a greater degree even.'

Wow! What a fantastic feeling it was to read that letter that morning. For the first time, I came to learn about a case similar to mine – and with talk of other cases, too. But hadn't the Royal Mail told me time and time again that I was the only one being prosecuted and that the problems had only come to light in my branch in Gaerwen? So, how many other cases were there then? Where were they? And had other postmasters been sent to jail as well? Those were the questions that went round and round in my head that morning as I read and reread Roch Garrard's letter, I don't know how many times in all. It was like manna from heaven for me, to be honest.

And then, a couple of weeks later, in this magical May, the third piece of the jigsaw fell into place. This came in the form of communication from the Welsh language TV current affairs programme, *Taro Naw*, and their two presenters, Anna Marie Robinson and Bryn Jones. The programme had heard about the *Computer Weekly* article and they had also heard about the case of Jo Hamilton in Hampshire and the connection we had made since then with Roch Garrard.

A couple of weeks later, they agreed to record an edition of *Taro Naw* about my case and it was arranged for me to travel down to Hampshire to meet Roch Garrard and Jo Hamilton, the sub-postmistress who had also been caught up in the whole affair. It was an amazing experience meeting up with the two of them that day, to exchange information and to discuss how we could move forward with our respective cases. We have maintained a close connection to this day. One of the good points to emerge from this whole nightmare is that I have met some amazing people and have made some excellent new friends along the way. There's always some good that can come out of even the worse situation, isn't there?

If I remember rightly, the *Taro Naw* programme itself was not actually shown on TV until 2010 for some reason, but when it did eventually appear it had been put together very well. I was extremely happy with the central theme of the programme, since it managed to sow some genuine seeds of doubt about how safe the Horizon system actually was and asked some tough questions about my own conviction and the convictions of other sub-postmasters, too. Many local people came up to me after watching the programme to express their support for me. It was as if that programme had allowed people to finally come out and say such things openly to me. In a way, it was odd that it had taken a TV show to enable so many people to express all this. The power of TV, indeed.

I remember Sian telling me: "Dad, ninety-five per cent of the people in Gaerwen know you are not guilty; there's only some five per cent who believe otherwise." And perhaps she was right on that. After all, she's been right on many things with this whole affair.

Some momentum was starting to build up by now and I had also got to know about the experiences of people such as Lee Castleton of Bridlington, who had been through exactly the same experiences as myself. Although Lee had suffered in a worse way since he had actually tried to challenge his case in a court, only to be judged guilty by the judge and slapped with costs of £300,000. He was subsequently bankrupted – like myself, of course.

It was like a rebirth for me in a way, a period of new possibilities and new awakenings, as I started to find out there was a whole lot more to the story than I had thought. At last, I was starting to feel there was some hope of clearing my name and find out exactly what had happened to all that money that had gone missing. I can remember turning to Eira and Sian one night and saying: "For the very first time, I think I'm going to win this one. And restore my good name at last."

Of course, I had no idea at the time how long this whole process was going to take over the coming years.

Sian

Those three events – Sion Tecwyn's visit, Roch Garrard's letter and the *Taro Naw* programme –were like coming across an oasis after being wandering through a dry and arid desert for two long years.

I have to pay a tribute here to Sion Tecwyn and Anna-Marie and Bryn Jones from the BBC for all their help. All three were very professional in their work and so helpful to us as a family.

Dealing with these three individuals was very helpful to me on a personal level as I had committed myself to get to the bottom of all this, if it was the very last thing I did. And this was essential in a way. I'm sure Dad would be very willing to admit that he often wanted to give up as things were so difficult. I really don't blame him for this in a way, with all the pressures that were upon him in so many ways. Dad needed someone to go in and bat for him on the very sticky wicket that he was facing. And I was the opening batsman, for sure, as well as the night watchman, too – especially with all the work I did in the evenings searching for information online.

It was all very scary for me since there was precious little help available from anywhere at this stage. It really was a matter of being thrown in at the deep end. 'Sink or swim', as they say. I had no knowledge about the law at all and yet I had to get up to speed on some of the basic elements – overnight, in a way.

One thing I did have in my favour was some local political background, which did prove to be helpful, especially as politics proved to be such an important element in the whole Post Office saga. I had helped out in the office of the local MP for Ynys Môn, Ieuan Wyn Jones, and undertaking some canvassing work for him during elections. I have always been a passionate Welshwoman wanting the best for Wales, so it was obvious that I would support Plaid Cymru – the Welsh nationalist party. It also helped that Ieuan Wyn Jones was such a lovely man to work for and so supportive of our family and what we were going through at the time.

Working for Ieuan Wyn Jones gave me some insight into the political scene in general and about all the shenanigans that went on in Westminster – and how much of a raw deal Wales was getting by being under their rule. Little did I think at the time how much such shenanigans would be replicated in the whole Post Office saga.

And where did I start with all this? Good question. It was a matter of searching on the internet for hours after coming home from work, looking for information – any form of information that could be helpful for us as a family. You have to remember here that we are talking about fifteen years ago, when there was a lot less information on the internet and not the glut of information we have at our fingertips through our mobile phones now. You also had much slower internet connections, which could be very frustrating – as I'm sure many will remember looking back at this period of time! Even so, I was finding some nuggets here and there that gave me and the whole family some real hope. It was also a huge help that we had connections in place with other sub-postmasters such as Lee Castleton and Jo Hamilton through the work we did with the *Taro Naw* TV show.

I'll never forget the evening that the *Taro Naw* programme was finally aired in 2010, with Dad, Mam and I sat together, holding hands on the sofa. Perhaps the most striking part of the programme was the map they showed that pinpointed where sub-postmasters had been prosecuted – dozens and dozens of them, with a huge cluster of cases in the Midlands. *Taro Naw* had been able to gather this crucial piece of information through the Freedom of Information Act.

Perhaps one of the best things ex PM Tony Blair did during his premiership was to introduce this act, which allowed members of the public to request information from public bodies, who are required by law to respond by a certain date. However, this is deeply ironic thinking in terms of his own involvement in the Post Office saga, which was to come to light later on at the public inquiry.

Anyway, going back to that night on the sofa, I remember jumping up with excitement once I saw that map on the screen. "Wow! Look how many people have been through exactly the same experience as you, Dad!" I shouted. I felt as if we had just won the lottery! Not money, but justice coming our way at long last.

In the wake of this programme, we also got to know about a more local case, which would play a big part in things for us over the next few years. It concerned sub-postmaster Alan Bates from Llandudno – one of the seven who were named in the initial report in *Computer Weekly* in May 2009. Alan was one of the very first to question the discrepancies with the Horizon system, refusing to make good on the losses that appeared in his branch. For this, he was sacked from his position by the Post Office. Dad became big mates with Alan Bates, who came to play a key role in the sub-postmasters campaign that was starting to kick off at this point. We are all looking forward to the ITV drama, *Mr Bates vs the Post Office*, which is to be aired on ITV early next year – and will also feature a cameo role for Dad and that awful first night for him in Walton Prison.

This connection with other sub-postmasters – Lee Castleton, Jo Hamilton and Alan Bates – was an absolute lifeline for us at this time. It made us all so overjoyed that there were other people who had gone through what we had gone through and knew what it was like, who could really empathise with our situation. We weren't alone anymore! The connection with the other sub-postmasters turned into a deep friendship, which has deepened as the years have gone on.

The Muse of Môn

The article in *Computer Weekly* on 9th May 2009 was a complete game changer. It was the result of an exhaustive six-month research project undertaken by their correspondent, Rebecca Thompson, which was published despite several legal threats against her and the magazine from the Royal Mail over the period of research.

The article mentioned the cases of the seven sub-postmasters they had researched: Lee Castleton, Jo Hamilton, Noel Thomas, Amar Baajaj, Alan Bates, Alan Brown and Julie Ford. The opening paragraph of the article was worded very carefully: "At least seven postmasters have come into conflict with the Post Office after the system showed losses which took them by surprise..."

Despite the softly-softly approach, there was no doubt about the impact of the story and the detailed information gathered about the seven individual postmasters. Mention was made of financial losses, loss of reputation and the serious mental anguish that came the way of the seven individuals and their families. The article focused in the main on Lee Castleton of Bridlington – the first sub-postmaster to be suspended as part of whole saga. Lee Castleton experienced exactly the same problems that befell Noel Thomas, although, in his case, he decided to challenge the Post Office's account in court.

He eventually lost his case in court, with the judge going as far as to say that he had no doubts whatsoever that it was Lee Castleton or one of his workers who was responsible for the losses of £23,000 in his own Post Office. Lee Castleton was then saddled with legal costs of £320,000 following the court case, with the disproportionately high figures totted up by the Post Office – a signal of how they intended to intimidate other sub-postmasters. Lee Castleton eventually had to declare himself to be bankrupt within two years.

Computer Weekly printed this response from the Post Office: '*Horizon is an extremely robust system which operates over our entire Post Office network and successfully records millions of transaction each day. There is no evidence that points to any fault with the technology.*'

The article signed off with what would turn out to be highly prophetic words by a senior officer with the Federation of Postmasters, who wanted to remain anonymous for the article: '*The problem we have here is the culture of the Post Office. It is heresy to say something can go wrong. No one can say computers cannot go wrong.*' The following years would show how accurate this description of the Post Office culture would turn out to be.

Noel

I have to say that all these developments with the Post Story were a huge help for me. My mood started to pick up and I was starting to get a taste for life again. At last! The old Noel was starting to return and I was starting to look forward to things, rather than looking back all the time and thinking how awful and hellish everything had been for so long, and how unfairly I had been treated by the system. All the constant negativity that had been such a constant presence in my life for three long years was starting to fade away, thank God.

One clear sign of this change in my spirit was the fact that I was, by 2010, feeling ready to go back to work – after three long years of not working at all. A mate of mine, Alan Hughes, mentioned to me that he could get me a job as a driver for the Yodel company delivering parcels and so on around the area. All I had to do was to buy a van and I would be ready to go. I followed his instructions and bingo! So, between 2010 and 2014, I delivered parcels around the area, in a manner that was very similar to my old job as a postman. The round actually included some of the villages that I had visited previously as a postie, such as Llanfairpwll, Gaerwen and Menai Bridge.

The pay wasn't all that good, to be honest, but it was a job and a reason to get up in the morning and have some order and some stability in my life. Seeing people and talking to people again on a daily basis was a huge part of the healing process for me. It made such a big difference to my mental health and my sense of self-worth, and it gave me a whole new insight into how important work is to all of us whatever we do in life. We have a saying in Welsh: '*Mewn gwaith mae gwynfyd*' ('Work brings blessings') – and it's so very true.

Being back in employment also seemed to steel me for the big task that lay ahead of trying to clear my name after my period behind bars – and to take all this to the next level in a way. Because, similar to my own personal state of being stuck, the whole Post

Office story seemed to be stuck as well. After the huge excitement in 2008 and those three significant episodes I mentioned earlier; things began moving at a snail's pace. Much too slow for my liking, I must admit.

Following the *Computer Weekly* story and some media follow-up by the London-based media, the Post Office started up a mediation process to see if there was a way to settle some of the problems that had come to light. However, after attending a couple of the meetings, I quickly came to see that these were completely useless. The meetings were delaying tactics on their part – a practice that developed into a whole way of operating throughout the whole saga. And which are still at play nearly a decade on – incredible as that may seem.

However, there were some positive developments during this period, such as the creation of the Justice for Sub-postmasters Alliance – a crew of sub-postmasters who had been affected by the prosecution cases – led by Alan Bates of Llandudno.

Alan has been like a tiger for us from the very start and has been a fantastic leader for all the wronged postmasters. It seems very appropriate that the ITV drama about the saga, which is to be aired next year, gives Alan the leading role in the production. Alan was sacked by the Post Office as he was unwilling to make good the supposed losses that had come to light in his branch in Llandudno and also because he had been very vocal in asking questions about the Horizon system when it was introduced in 2000.

Alan was the one who set up a meeting for around thirty sub-postmasters in a village called Kennington in the Midlands in 2011. I was driven down to this meeting by my cousin, Gordon, who lives in Bontnewydd. Gordon is another member of the family who has stuck by my side from the very start and always been supportive of me.

This meeting proved to be such an eye-opener for me, hearing so many other sub-postmasters sharing their stories and their experiences, which were so, so similar to my own story. I can't begin to tell you how much of a vindication it was for me to hear all these stories at this meeting. That original story in *Computer Weekly* about the 'secret seven' had now opened out to include many more people. It was not so secret anymore – it was all coming out into broad daylight.

As Alan Bates spoke so well at this first meeting, he was chosen to be the chair of this new campaigning group. He proved himself to be very effective in the role, as well as being very supportive to the rest of us in the group. You could always pick up the phone to Alan and feel better after talking to him, such was his enthusiasm and his charisma as an individual. It was very apt that Alan's name would be the lead name on the group litigation we would eventually bring as sub-postmasters against the Post Office in the High Court some years down the line in 2019.

Sian

Seeing Dad back in work again was just such a heart-warming experience for us all as a family. The job with Yodel gave him back his dignity and a sense of purpose in life. And also, of course, gave him something to take his mind off all the other problems that were still there for him.

Mam, Arfon, Edwin and I really felt that Dad had found himself again and that we had found him again as well in a way. At last, he was stepping out of the dark pit he had been trapped in for so much time. Getting a job again seemed to tell him: 'There's a place for you again in our local community. You are wanted, you are included, you are valued.' Words that Dad had longed to hear for so, so long.

I remember turning to him after he'd been in the job for a couple of weeks and saying: "Wow, Dad, this has changed everything for us. We are all so much happier as a family seeing you working again."

And Dad responding: "Well, yes, not being under your feet all day here has been a big help for all of us!"

The old banter and leg-pulling, which was so much part of who he was, was starting to reappear as well. Yes, of course, there were still bad days and Dad was drawn back into what had been done to him, as well as a sense of despair that things were so slow in moving on in resolving things. In general, though, we were in a whole new territory now, so to speak.

Over these years, I worked in a number of different organisations: a local building merchants, the office of the local MP, a community housing organisation and a care home. This work kept me busy during the day. I'd come home, have a bite to eat and then I'd start on my second job, as I called it, going on the internet to try and find out whatever I could about the Post Office saga. I'd be the first to admit that this became a complete obsession for me. I was like a dog with a bone. The need to clear Dad's name and achieve justice for him was like my food and drink during this time. In a way, it was fortunate that I was single at this time, after my marriage had broken up some years previously, so I was able to devote all my spare time to the cause.

It was also a huge boost for me that I became close friends with Alan Bates, Lee Castleton and Jo Hamilton, along with a number of other sub-postmasters, too. We all became like an extended family in a way, helping each other, supporting each other and sustaining each other. All of us felt we were part of a great crusade on behalf of our respective families and fighting against this monstrosity – The Post Office – that had turned our lives upside down.

As time wore on, we came to see that we were fighting against an even bigger monster – i.e. several Westminster Governments who had been intimately involved in the scandal throughout the whole period in question. This was to make our struggle even more difficult.

The Muse of Môn
Following the publicity in *Computer Weekly* and other newspapers as well, the Post Office story was starting to come to more and more people's attention throughout the UK. The year 2012 was a

key turning point since this was the year when the Post Office put an end to the process of prosecuting sub-postmasters for financial losses in their accounts after prosecuting over seven hundred of them over a period of ten years.

By this year, a distinct political aspect was also beginning to make itself felt in the whole process: a dimension that, in truth, was merely the continuation of a process that reached back to the very start of the whole saga. We have to remember it was Tony Blair's New Labour Government who insisted that the Post Office implement the Horizon computerised system, which belonged to the huge Japanese conglomerate, Fujitsu. Apparently, Blair was desperate to keep the Japanese Government onboard for other reasons and the Fujitsu programme had to go ahead, whatever the cost and whatever reservations or concerns might have been raised at the time. With the public inquiry still ongoing, Tony Blair's role in the whole saga has been highlighted with calls for him to be called to the inquiry itself in its latter stages, so that his exact role in the process can be examined fully.

2012 was also a significant year because the Royal Mail business was sold to the private sector, with the Post Office counters service kept in public hands, coming under the control of the Department for Business, Innovation and Skills (BIS). In 2016, BIS became part of BEIS (Department for Business, Energy and Industrial Strategy). This department was soon alerted to the Horizon problem as the matter was raised by different MPs in Westminster, such as Albert Owen, Noel Thomas's own MP for Ynys Môn.

On 8th August 2012, Albert Owen received a letter from the Liberal Democrat MP Norman Lamb, who was, at that stage, the Minister for BIS. The letter made reference to an external review that was to be undertaken on the Horizon system.

Lamb's words seem to summarise the entire mentality of the Post Office at the time and suggests how much weight such an external review would carry in reality.

'*Post Office Ltd (POL) remains fully confident about the robustness and integrity of its Horizon system and related accounting processes. Over the past ten years, many millions of branch reconciliations have been carried out with transactions and balances accurately recorded on Horizon by more than 25,000 different postmasters in total,'* he wrote.

As part of this review, a company of forensic accountants, Second Sight, were commissioned to undertake this work. It later transpired that their critical report was subsequently hidden away by the Post Office and never published. This, in turn, became the subject of a Panorama investigation, with the programme's presenter, John Sweeney, coming up to interview Noel with a copy of the report (leaked by a whistle-blower) in his hand. Second Sight's investigators were unsparing in their conclusions, declaring that Post Office officials *'fail to identify the underlying cause of shortfall prior to initiating civil recovery action or criminal proceedings.'* And even more damning was their assertion that *'investigators seem to have found that recording admissions of false accounting was the key to achieving rapid and inexpensive asset recovery.'*

The tide was slowly starting to turn and, in 2015, a parliamentary debate was held in Westminster at last. Some of the contributions made in that debate were explosive to say the least. One of the most critical MPs was Andrew Bridgen, the Conservative MP for North West Leicestershire. He referred to a statement by a spokesperson on behalf of the Post office saying they were sorry that some of their staff had experienced 'lifestyle problems' after working in Post Offices: *'We have to wonder whether the organisation is even aware of the misery it has caused. The fact that Post Office Ltd believes that honest, decent, hard-working people losing their homes, businesses, their savings, reputation and, worst of all, in some cases their liberty can be quantified as "lifestyle changes" only serves to show that the organisation is not fit to conduct an inquiry into the matter.'*

Andrew Bridgen was one of the very first to call for a judicial review of the Horizon system, declaring it was not possible to trust the Post Office to conduct an investigation that was truly honest and transparent. 'The management style of the senior management at the Post office is Dickensian and they have almost a feudal relationship with their sub-postmasters. This is now a national scandal. The Post Office have demonstrated that it is incapable of putting its own house in order, so it falls to this house and to the government to do it,' he said.

Kevan Jones, the Labour MP for Durham North was equally scathing in his assessment of the situation: '*The fundamental point is this: who controls the Post Office? This organisation is out of control. It has led to people's lives being ruined and, as we have heard, in some cases, to people being given prison sentences when clearly they are innocent.*'

These damning words were met with a muted response from George Freeman, the Under-Secretary for Life Sciences on behalf of the Conservative Government. To all intents and purposes, he ignored the words of both Andrew Bridgen and Kevan Jones as he praised the Post Office to the high heavens for their programme to invest in their branches and develop the business for the future. This showed once again how resistant different governments proved themselves to face the whole problem honestly, even though they were directly involved in setting the strategic direction of the Post Office and monitoring its progress via its representative on the Post Office Board of Directors and Audit and Risk Committee from 2012 onwards.

A succession of government ministers (representing both the Tories and the Liberal Democrats) held the Postal Services brief over these years, including Ed Davey, Norman Lamb, Jo Swinson, Baroness Neville-Rolfe, Margot James, Andrew Griffiths and Kelly Tolhurst, with not a single one of them willing to properly examine the fast-developing public scandal involving their own departmental brief.

But despite all the empty words from both the Post Office and the government, it was becoming increasingly clear to many more people that there was something seriously wrong with the

Post Office's Horizon system and that many innocent people had suffered huge injustices in the wake of these deficiencies. All of this was to come to some kind of crescendo over the next few years.

Noel

This proved to be a very revealing period of time, but also a very frustrating one in many aspects.

I met up with so many other sub-postmasters who had endured exactly the same experiences as myself, with all of us in agreement that problems with the computerised system had to be at the root of all the problems. The same story was repeated by every single one of us. It was just incredible. Like that film *Groundhog Day*, in a way, with every aspect being repeated time and time again. The UK Media were also starting to run with it, with *Computer Weekly* running regular stories on the saga and the *Daily Mail* also starting to provide regular coverage to our case as postmasters.

It was very ironic to see a Tory paper like the *Daily Mail* leading the way on this, with the *Daily Mirror* – supposedly a paper for the workers – not giving the story any attention at all! It really did come to something, that I – an ordinary Welshman – had to become an avid reader of the *Daily Mail* to find out what was going on with the saga. The journalist Tom Witherow, now with *The Times*, wrote some excellent articles for the *Daily Mail* and I was fortunate enough to be interviewed by him a couple of time as well.

It proved a huge disappointment for me personally that the *Daily Post*, our regional paper here in north Wales, also ignored the story entirely. I still don't understand how they managed to ignore it for so long, even when it was picking up steam and gaining attention on a UK level. I'd really like an explanation from the *Daily Post* one day as to why they chose to ignore such a huge story with such a strong local angle. Was there an instruction from above – from the parent company, Trinity Mirror – that they were not supposed to touch the story? Questions, questions. And so many questions still unanswered to this day, of course.

At the time, though, I was trying to focus on the positive and the tremendous coverage that was being provided elsewhere. The high point of this was the book eventually written by the journalist Nick Wallis, who attended daily throughout both trials of the Group Litigation Order at the High Court and interviewed each one of the affected sub-postmasters in turn. All of this proved to be great material for his brilliant book, *The Great Post Office Scandal*, which was published in 2021.

So, in a media sense, the tide was starting to turn in many ways, but this couldn't be said about the Post Office itself. They were dragging their feet at every turn, postponing, deferring, delaying, deflecting on every possible occasion. This behaviour was to become their default setting for the years to come. For my part, my eyes were being opened wider and wider to see the full extent of what this whole scandal amounted to.

Politicians across the political spectrum were deeply involved and implicated in it all. The truth is that all parties were up to their necks in it: the Labour Party, as it was Tony Blair who had insisted the system be pushed onto the Post Office at the end of the nineties; and then the Tories/Lib Dems, who had been running things since 2010; and then the Tories alone from 2015. BIS was a government department that was actually responsible for the Post, but they didn't want to be responsible at all for what had happened.

As it was a period of time that involved waiting for answers that weren't forthcoming, I had to develop a good deal of patience and perseverance. One factor that definitely helped me get through all this was the fact that I had a new job by 2014. I had enjoyed my time with Yodel, delivering parcels around the south of the island, but when the office moved to Llandudno, things started to go south and I was getting a lot less money for each parcel delivered. Things came to a head when they stopped paying us completely.

Luckily for me, I happened to know Richard and Michelle Gould who ran the Holland Arms Gardening Centre in a village close to Gaerwen. He approached me one day to ask whether I would be interested in working with them for a day or two every week. As I was a big gardener myself, this was an offer that was too good to refuse, so I accepted the offer very thankfully.

I enjoyed my employment at Holland Arms very much. My hours increased as the weeks went on and it ended up that I was working there for 4 days a week by the end, which suited me down to a T. My old people skills seemed to be flowing back every day I was at Holland Arms, since it is a place where so many people from all over the island visit, and I was in my element chatting to people from all over and helping them to choose their plants etc. I had so many chats about my experiences in prison and the whole Post Office saga, especially as more information was reaching public awareness through the media etc.

I remember Richard turning to me one day and saying, "Is there anyone you don't know, Noel?!" He couldn't believe that I knew so many people all across the island, but I think he was secretly very happy about it since it was all good PR for Holland Arms.

I was counting my blessings at this time. After losing my job with Yodel and with the whole business with the Post taking an eternity to move forward, it could have been very easy for me to slip back into a deep pit of depression. But now, I had been blessed with a job I liked, in my own area, and I was once again able to talk and relate to people on an everyday basis as before. I only gave up my role with Holland Arms at Christmas 2021. I was seventy-five at that point and I thought it was a good time to retire. You have to remember that the job involved a good deal of carrying heavy pots and the like, which could be quite demanding.

Although I was in very good health overall, by that time my body was saying, "Enough is enough," so I decided it was time to pack it in, counting my blessings for the experiences and all the new friendships that were made at Holland Arms over those years.

I was also blessed, of course, by having my family living around me and being so supportive at all times. Being a *taid* ('grandfather') was a role that gave me great deal of pleasure and purpose, and I loved taking an active part in the lives of Arthur Huw and Mared, the children of Edwin and Gail, and Jade, the child of Arfon, as they were growing up. Auntie Gwenda in nearby Llangefni was also an important part of our family, too, and I had a great deal of support from her whenever I went over to see her. Auntie Gwenda is Eira's twin sister, as mentioned, and the two make a formidable duo. I have to make sure I'm out the back whenever Auntie Gwenda comes over for a chat with Eira in the house here – as I know I won't have a chance between the two of them! There were also my cousins, who I could depend on, such as Medwyn in Llanfairpwll, Gordon in Bontnewydd and Joan (who had still kept her Welsh up to a very high level, despite living in Solihull for many years), who were also a key part of the supportive family jigsaw.

I also have to mention the good friends we had at this time and two special friends from my time with Ynys Môn County Council, who were particularly loyal and stayed true through thick and thin – Councillor Eurfryn Davies of Llandegfan and Councillor Trefor Lloyd Hughes from Holyhead.

In 2016, we finally heard that things were moving on for us as sub-postmasters, as the Criminal Cases Review Commission (CCRC) had agreed to review our cases again and assess the whole effectiveness of the Horizon system as part of this review. This gave us real hope since the next step could well mean referring the cases on to the High Court in London.

I got a phone call from Alan Bates in Llandudno, who had showed such a warrior spirit fighting on our behalf. He said: "Noel, this is the real thing. Now that the CCRC are involved, it's only a matter of time, because we can take this whole thing to the High Court and clear all of our names."

"Are you sure Alan?" I said, since a kind of cynicism had been hardwired into me when it came to matters with the Post Office.

"Believe me, Noel," Alan answered. "This is a hell of a big breakthrough for us. We are on the path to victory now!" And then he added triumphantly, "Finally!"

And Alan was right to trust his instincts. From that point onwards, things started to move forward much quicker.

Following the consultation between the CCRC and the Justice for Sub-postmasters Alliance, it was decided that there was enough evidence for a group litigation against the Post Office in the High Court. The purpose of this group litigation was, through a sequence of trials, to expose the integrity of the Horizon system, to demonstrate how this may well have been the root cause of discrepancies in branch accounts and to challenge the sub-postmaster contract by which they were held liable for all losses in their branch accounts.

A legal firm by the name of Freeths agreed to take on the case on a 'no win, no fee' basis. This Group Litigation Order was finally presented in the High Court in 2017 with my name as one of the lead claimants and all the cases to be considered by a leading judge by the name of Mr Justice Fraser. He divided the considered evidence into two trials, termed 'Common Issues' and 'Horizon Issues', with the Post Office fighting the case at every step of the way. And in doing so, spending £100million of taxpayers' money in what eventually proved to be defending the indefensible. Even trying to 'recuse' the judge (to have him removed from the proceedings) was promptly refused by another court.

It took two years in all, but by the end of 2019, the Post Office finally came to an agreement with Freeths, the legal firm representing the 555 postmasters. They finally threw in the towel and agreed to pay compensation to the postmasters for the injustice that had been delivered to us. A sum of £57 million was agreed. It was an amazing day, I can tell you. A day that I had been waiting for, for such a long time. And praying for, too.

There was a huge celebration in our home in Gaerwen that night, as you can well imagine! The news obviously triggered a huge amount of interest locally, of course: "Noel, you're a millionaire now. What are you going to do with all that money?" was the question I was asked by so many. But what people didn't realise at the time was that the lion's share of this compensation – eighty per cent of it, no less – was swallowed up in the claimant's legal and funding costs to Freeths and also Therium, the third-party funders who took on the risk of financing the case.

After 80 per cent of the £57 million went on fees, the rest of the money was then divided among all the postmasters. I got £11,000, so I was very far away from being anything close to a millionaire! And to be honest with you, most of this money went on paying different costs I had incurred anyway. I've lost count of how many times I had to explain this to people in the village and beyond. No, there was no luxury yacht, luxury cruise or any luxuries at all lined up for me despite that headline-grabbing total.

No doubt the £11,000 was a valuable sum, of course, and a help to myself and the family after having lived on next to nothing for a number of years, but it's important to state here that this court case was all about clearing us as a group of sub-postmasters. There was another important step yet to be taken, of course: clearing my own individual name in a court of law. This was the next step and it would take another two years to achieve.

Sian

This was an extremely busy time for me. I was still continuing with my crash course in legal matters relating to Dad's case online every single night, on top of my own day job. All the information I had to deal with tended to fry my brain at times, but, in this respect, I was very lucky to have this support family to help me, in the form of the other sub-postmasters we had now come to know. We actually set up a support group for each other on WhatsApp, with around thirty of us on there. I found this to be invaluable in so many different ways since there was so much resting on my shoulders in all of this.

Dad would be the first to admit that he has no idea whatsoever about new media – where there's so much information available for the ordinary citizen – and he had to depend completely on me to keep him up to date about what was going on. He started jokingly referring to me as the 'home secretary' – and the 'home secretary' certainly had her work cut out for her during this period of time, as there were messages flooding in from all directions: from the Ynys Môn MP Albert Owen, the Criminal Cases Review Commission who were reviewing Dad's case and requests for information and reviews from different journalists, too. One of these was the journalist Nick Wallis, who reported daily from both trials at the High Court and followed every conviction of individual sub-postmasters as they were overturned. Nick Wallis then went on to write *The Great Post Office Scandal*, which was published in 2021.

Taro Naw – the Welsh language current affairs programme – were also keeping in touch with us, as well as the BBC's flagship *Panorama* show. Indeed, one of its top presenters, John Sweeney, came to Gaerwen twice to interview Dad for a programme they aired on the scandal.

You won't believe this, but at one point I had 34,000 emails in my inbox relating to the whole matter. 34,000! Thankfully, all of these have been safely backed up.

As you can imagine, my head was almost exploding with all the information I had to read and process. I also had to exercise some discretion in what exactly I would present to Dad and Mam during this process. Obviously, I wanted to keep them in the loop, but I didn't want to confuse them too much with all the ins and outs, so to speak. I also wanted to keep their spirits up throughout this emotional roller coaster and attempt to convince them that we would win at the end of the day.

Mind you, I did have my own serious doubts about this at many stages, especially with the Post Office playing all their mind games with us constantly, which also played on my mind with so many sleepless nights trying to figure it all out. However, I had to put a brave face on and present a positive spin in front of Dad and Mam. It was almost as if a role-reversal of sorts had happened in our relationship and I was now the parent figure, having to look out for them, care for them and monitor their situation constantly.

All this strain was playing havoc with the rest of my life. As I've said before, I was single at that stage, which at least freed up a lot of time to devote myself to Dad's case, but any social life was on the back burner completely. My friends would often ask: "Sian, come out with us for a meal or a drink."

My automatic response would always be: "Sorry, I can't. I've got work to do on Dad's case."

"Oh not again Sian!" they would always say.

I would just shrug my shoulders and reply: "Sorry, girls, it's just what it is right now."

I was single, but I was also becoming single-minded with all this as well. And as I was living with my parents at Rhos Ellen as well, it was just consuming my whole life. It wasn't a natural state of affairs, I know, but under the circumstances, there was nothing else to be done. I just had to put my head down, wait and pray that things would resolve themselves and that we could have a sense of normality again in our lives.

We took a step towards that normality when the Criminal Cases Review Commission announced in 2017 that the case of the sub-postmasters could be sent to the High Court. At last there was real hope that we could finally achieve some justice. The first trial, the Common Issues Trial began in the High Court in November 2018, with the overall settlement reached in the same court in December 2019. I remember that day as if it were yesterday.

Edwin, my brother, and I were, at that time, working in the Fairways Nursing Home in a nearby village and we had been alerted by Freeths, the solicitors representing the sub-postmasters, that a judgement was due that day. We were on tenterhooks all morning, not able to concentrate on our work at all, just wondering and wondering what was going on and what had been announced by the judges. There was no word from Dad or anybody else for that matter as to what had happened.

"Edwin," I told my brother at lunchtime. "I can't stand all this tension. And being in the dark about this all morning. I'll just have to phone Freeths myself to find out what's going on."

So, I phoned Freeths, who said that Dad had actually received a message from them just after 9am to tell him that the group litigation had won. Dad, being the technophobe that he is, hadn't opened his email that morning and simply didn't know that he and the others had won the case! Typical Dad! I phoned him to share the good news and told him to check his email. And there we were, the three of us – Dad, Edwin and myself – crying a river down the phone with each other for a good while. The tears continued to flow that day as I let other members of the family and close friends know about the judgement.

After fourteen years of fighting and campaigning, after all the trauma, all the tears, all the frustrations, all the endless twists and turns, we had finally won the day. '*Haleliwia*', as we say in Welsh!

There was another two years before we could clear Dad's name as an individual as the High Court case was just a group judgement, but we all knew this was just a matter of time now.

The final victory was coming.

The Muse of Môn

The judgements issued by Mr Justice Fraser in the High Court at the end of 2019 were extremely detailed and were handed down separately: 'Common Issues' in March 2019 (315 pages) and 'Horizon Issues' in December 2019 (313 pages).

He delivered some scathing comments about the Post Office throughout the whole saga, describing their way of operating as 'oppressive behaviour' at one point. In referring to the Post Office's description of themselves on their website as 'The nation's most trusted brand', he had this to say: "As far as these claimants and the subject matter of this Group Litigation is concerned, this might be thought to be wholly wishful thinking."

He revealed that the evidence that had been presented to him showed that Horizon contained thirty bugs and other deficiencies that could – and did – cause substantial losses in innumerable Post Office branches all over the UK. He further stated that there were no grounds at all to the Post Office's oft-repeated mantra that the Horizon system was completely dependable. "It was not remotely robust," he said. "The number, extent and type of impact of the numerous bugs, errors and defects I have found in Legacy Horizon makes this clear."

He added in his judgement that it was clear that the Post Office and Fujitsu (the Japanese company responsible for Horizon) had been fully aware of serious problems with the system for a good period of time, but had decided to deny everything, as there was: "a distinct sensitivity within both the Post Office and Fujitsu about keeping this information to themselves in order to avoid a 'loss of confidence' in Horizon and the integrity of its data. A less complimentary (though accurate) way of putting it would be to enable the Post Office to continue to assert the integrity of Horizon and avoid publicly acknowledging the presence of a software bug."

We can infer from Judge Fraser's Horizon Issues judgement that all cases against sub-postmasters issued by different courts that relied on Horizon evidence should be considered unsafe. This judgement opened the gates for all those who had been convicted on Horizon evidence, whether or not they were one of the 555, to take their cases to the Court of Appeal to be overturned if they could convince the CCRC and the Court of Appeal that their convictions were unsafe. As this book was going to print, some ninety one sub-postmasters have been cleared in this way.

These were the main points made by Mr Justice Fraser in his judgement. In the list below, POL stands for 'Post Office Limited' and SPMs stands for 'sub-postmasters':

- Legacy Horizon was not 'robust' in any way.
- There was a substantial and material risk of mistakes in

the accounts of Post Office branches because of bugs, deficiencies and mistakes in the Horizon system.

- Independent testimony supported what the SPMs were saying, including testimony submitted by the Post Office's own engineers and accountants.
- POL had failed to reveal to SPMs the real and correct situation as to the reliability of Horizon.
- POL and Fujitsu had automatically assumed that it must be the SPMs who were responsible for the financial discrepancies. The level of research undertaken by the two companies into this matter had been negligible.
- The SPMs had been placed at a considerable disadvantage by not being able to have access to relevant information that might have helped them to research into the financial losses and challenge these.
- The SPMs had no means to challenge losses within Horizon.
- POL had overstressed the necessity placed upon SPMs to make good for any losses that appeared.
- 'Remote access' to branch accounts from Fujitsu was widespread and indeed some branch accounts had been changed without SPMs being aware of this.

This 'remote access' – i.e. Fujitsu's ability to change Post Office accounts from their base in Swindon – became a moot issue in the inquiry, which started its public hearings in February 2022, after a senior officer within the company stated that the Post Office knew about all this from the outset.

Mr Justice Fraser's judgement was truly shocking on so many levels. It proved in essence that the legal processes against sub-postmasters, which extended back over almost twenty years, had been completely flawed from the start. And even worse, that this was allowed to fester for many years, even though senior people knew full well that the whole process was flawed.

It was very revealing that Mr Justice Fraser had shared the blame for the whole saga equally between the Post Office and Fujitsu in his judgement. Over the years, Fujitsu had stayed in the shadows to a large extent with the Post Office being the public face of the whole story. But Mr Justice Fraser now suggested very clearly that it was not feasible for Fujitsu to hide behind the Post Office brand any further and that they had to take their full share of the blame for the fiasco. And the role of the big Japanese company was to come more and more into the public consciousness over the years to come. Not only in the individual cases brought before the Court of Appeal in 2021, but also in the public inquiry under the chairmanship of Sir Wyn Williams, which began its public stage in February 2022.

If the Post Office and Fujitsu were now being horribly exposed, it was also a damning judgement on the whole legal system itself and on those who were associated with this system in different ways. But dragging into the public domain a glimpse of the dark and fiercely protected vested interests of this corporate world – blessed by governments and facilitated by lawyers – has been a painfully slow process. Our understanding of the ways in which commercial, reputational and political interests interacted and actively delayed justice is only just beginning.

In 2019, victory at the High Court meant that a reckoning for the Post Office, Fujitsu and for the legal system itself was just starting to take shape.

CHAPTER 8

Clearing My Name at Long Last

Noel

Once we had that judgement in the High Court, my mind automatically started to think about the next step. Yes, clearing our names as one big group of sub-postmasters was brilliant, but, for me personally, there would be no rest until I had cleared my name as an individual.

I was quite confident that the next step in the process would happen in view of what the solicitors were telling us, but we would have to wait another six months to know for definite that this was going to take place. Once again, the CCRC (Criminal Cases Review Commission) was a central part of this process, sending me a letter to confirm that they believed there was enough evidence to take my case to the Court Of Appeal.

This was the wording of the CCRC's decision in the above-mentioned letter:

i)   Gaining dependable information from Horizon was essential for both the prosecution and sentencing, and without that in place, there was no way the process could be a fair one.

ii) It was a stain on the public conscience that the appellant had faced a prosecution.

Receiving this letter was a red-letter day in our house! At last I was going to get my day in court and it would be totally different to that farce of a day in 2006 when I was sent down. I felt that a huge weight had finally been lifted off my shoulders. There was a spring in my step and a new vigour and confidence in my walks around the village, with my head held higher as I went on my way. I just knew that justice was coming.

Even though we didn't have a definite date at that point, there was a lot of work to be done. In the first place, we had to find a new set of solicitors to represent us in the Court of Appeal. Personally, I would have been very happy to continue with Freeths – the company who had represented us in the High Court – because I felt they had done an excellent job on our behalf. However, according to the law of the land, as they had won a case representing us in one court – the High Court – they did not have the right to then represent us in another court – the Court of Appeal. Therefore, we had to find another company entirely, which could have been a lengthy and complicated process. Fortunately, though, we had Alan Bates on the case. Not only was Alan a tiger fighting for us in the public eye, he was always ready to perform the less glamorous stuff in the background on our behalf as well. Before long, he had found a company called Hudgells of Hull, who were willing to represent us in the Court of Appeal. He had to submit a formal application to Hudgells with this, but this was soon accepted and we were on our way.

Neil Hudgell would represent thirty-three of us as sub-postmasters in the Court of Appeal in 2021 – these were the first batch of sub-postmasters who were wrongly charged by the Post Office – and Alan Bates chose well. Neil came over to Gaerwen to meet me and I took to him immediately. He's a lad from a working-class background like myself, who was raised by his grandmother in Hull. Neil worked himself up over the years to own a legal firm in the city. It's also a firm that prides itself on giving opportunities for young local men and women, which impressed me a huge amount, I must say – I've always got my ex-county councillor hat on in some way, always worrying about the lack of opportunities for young men and young women on Ynys Môn and the fact that we are losing so much talent because of a lack of employment locally.

Neil is very rooted in his community and a big rugby league fan. Indeed, he was the owner of Hull Kingston Rovers Rugby League Club at one point. I've got nothing to say about the game myself, to be honest, but Neil is always talking about the sport and inviting Sian and myself to go up to Hull to watch a game with him. We'll have to go one of these days!

After that first meeting, Hudgells were in regular contact with us over the next few months by means of the phone, email and zoom to let us know how things were moving ahead. And once again, it was the 'home secretary' who had to manage this process! Thank God she is so able. I would have been floored having to handle all this correspondence, which seemed to arrive from different directions every single day.

The bulk of the legal work had been done by Freeths for the initial case, of course, but Hudgells had to update matters and ensure that all the relevant facts were at the tips of his fingertips for the new case. And they proved to be very thorough and meticulous throughout. Neil Hudgell also proved himself to be very supportive of us on a personal level, being a very personable and likeable individual to deal with.

Knowing that Hudgells were doing all the necessary background work for us at this point, it was fairly easy for me just to continue with my usual day-to-day life. Being with my family, working at the garden centre and continuing to do the things I enjoyed so much, chatting and engaging with people in my local area – and looking forward to the big day, whenever that would arrive.

Sian

Between everything, those years from 2019 to 2021 proved to be a roller-coaster experience for us as a family – yet another one. The whole Covid saga in 2020 placed even greater pressure on myself personally as I had, by then, started working in the reception at a local nursing home, Fairways, not far from our home in Gaerwen. And we all know what happened in so many nursing homes during that time. On top of all this general stress, a family tragedy was to devastate us.

Things had all started out on such a high in this period as a result of the High Court Judgement, which saw Dad, along with 555 other sub-postmasters, cleared in a group litigation case. Then we had the news from the CCRC that Dad's individual case would be progressing to the Court of Appeal. I had to be contact point for our family with Neil Hudgell from Hull, the solicitor who would be representing us at the Court of Appeal. Neil would become an important member of our family over this next period, providing a regular stream of advice, guidance and support as we prepared for our date with destiny. This all added to the huge learning exercise that came my way during the long and drawn-out process of trying to clear Dad's name.

Social media was becoming a huge factor in society and with all the material being posted and shared about this whole matter online, the temperature was rising all the time. Neil would always tell me to keep clear of the worse bickering that could go on between people online. "Sian," he would tell me often. "Don't join in with all that. Keep a low profile, if you can. It will be better for all of us in the long run."

Neil's main concern was that some of the comments and observations being made online about the whole Post Office affair could endanger our success chances in the Court of Appeal. Very wise advice, as it turned out. "Remember, Sian," he would tell me. "The Post Office are probably trawling through all these comments looking for things that could be used against us, so let's be careful!"

And that's exactly the same advice he's given us more recently, as the public inquiry develops under the chairmanship of Sir Wyn Williams.

There's a lot of very useful and important material posted on social media that has undoubtedly helped our case, but there's a lot of needless bickering and arguments on there as well, and sometimes things can go overboard. I personally can be a bit passionate about things – being a typical redhead! – and it was very handy to have Neil at hand to tell me every now and then: "Sian! Cool down and come off Twitter for a while. Let the process sort itself out." Some good advice for all of us, I think!

Well, 2020 arrived, didn't it, and changed everything for everyone. As I mentioned earlier, by this point I was working at the Fairways nursing home, along with my brother, Edwin. Edwin was working there as a chef and I was working on the reception desk, and it was nice to have his company. But it proved to be a dreadfully difficult year there, especially with the lockdowns, and the effects those lockdowns had on the residents at the home and their families.

Many of the residents were unable to see their families and that, of course, made life almost insufferable for them. Without being able to see their families, many of them were just withering away emotionally and physically. To a large degree, because of the general situation, we – as staff – became both their helpers and their families. And even though my official role was at the reception desk, my job became much more than this during this awful time for all of us.

I'm very similar to my Dad in the sense that I am a people person and these skills became essential at this point. I had to step up in some way. When I was working some long shifts at the nursing home, I used to go around last thing at night to say goodnight to all the residents and they really appreciated this small gesture of mine. After all, hadn't they lost all connection with their families because of the Covid rules, which were so disheartening and demoralising for their emotional health and their physical health alike? This period took a heavy toll on many of them, it must be said.

Being on the frontline in the nursing home dealing with Covid, which affected older, more vulnerable people primarily, was so very tough. Nursing and care work like this is always difficult, of course, but it was so much tougher at that time. Over the coming year, we lost a number of the home's residents to Covid and I found this very hard to deal with as I had become so close to them and I thought the world of them.

2020 was just a very, very odd year for everyone, with all our lives turned upside down because of the Covid saga. The process of having to adjust to wearing masks, keeping our distance from people, lockdowns and all the rest of it was just a huge shift and changed all our lives. Everybody was living in a state of fear and anxiety – ramped up the mass media – and all this stress proved to be so difficult for everyone. It's odd looking back at it all now and thinking about how much it changed everything. Forever, in a way.

The only saving grace was that we had a lengthy spell of good weather during the spring and summer of 2020, along with an unusual sense of peace and quiet all around. There was much less traffic on the roads and the tourist industry ground to a halt, to all intents and purposes. It was an amazing sense of having our island back for ourselves for those few months. It gave us an idea of how life used to be before tourism became so all-powerful here. Tourism is important for an island like Ynys Môn, of course, but there is a very real feeling now among any local people that it's reached some kind of saturation point with too many cars and too many people pouring in and affecting the quality of life for those who actually live here. So, this pause was a relief for many locals, although we knew it couldn't last forever.

By the end of 2020, we had received the date for Dad's hearing in the Court of Appeal. The evidence was to be heard over four days in the Court of Appeal on 19th-22nd March, with the judgement to be delivered by the three Law Lords on Friday 23rd April. This was a definite target for us to aim for as a family, but it wouldn't be possible to finish talking about 2020 without talking about another crisis that came out of nowhere to rock us as a family. A crisis that was to shake our whole world.

Noel

2020 was a bittersweet year – a particularly bittersweet year for us as a family. After all the trauma we had been through along the years, we were looking forward to an end to it all and getting our lives back. Little did we know that another family tragedy, an even worse tragedy, was about to engulf us.

Arfon, our eldest son, had been earning a living as a painter and decorator for many years, travelling to different places, including over the border in England. By the end of 2019, Arfon started to complain about pain in his arm and not being able to raise it properly. He went in for an MRI scan at Ysbyty Gwynedd in February 2020 and was given the terrible news that he had stage 4 cancer. This news was a hammer blow for me. There are no words to describe how I felt at the time. A complete sense of numbness and waves of dark, dark feelings swept over me yet again. Was there any escape at all from this continuing nightmare over our little family for so many years? What had we done to deserve all this misfortune?

Some radiotherapy treatments were arranged for Arfon at Ysbyty Glan Clwyd, another hospital down the Welsh coast, but he would continue to live with us at Rhos Ellen, Gaerwen, between his bouts of treatment. The next nine weeks were an absolute hell for us as a family, having to watch Arfon going downhill so quickly, and seeing him weakening and declining every single day.

Arfon wasn't the best at sharing his feelings with us as a family – very similar to me in a way – and if you wanted to know what was going on with him, you had to take him out for a pint more often than not. Unfortunately, during this period, he was just too weak and ill to do that even. All of us were so sad and frustrated that we weren't able to help him in any way.

Again, I have to raise my cap to Sian here since she was wonderful with Arfon, nursing him and ensuring he took the tablets he needed to ease some of the pain and so on. But despite all her efforts, there was no recovery in Arfon's case and he was taken away from us on 26th March 2020. He was only fifty. It was a heart-breaking experience for myself and Eira as his parents and for everyone else in our family, of course.

What made things so much worse somehow was that we had enjoyed such joy as a family with the High Court in 2019, but now we were thrown back into a pit of deep despair again. Poor Arfon, who had been so supportive of me throughout the Post Office saga, was not allowed to live to see the big day when I was cleared on an individual level by the Appeal Court in 2021. And because this took place at the start of Covid, we didn't really feel that Arfon was given any justice in death and his funeral either. Being such a popular lad, one would have expected several hundreds at his funeral to say their last farewells, but because of the Covid rules in place at the time, only eighteen of us were allowed to attend the crematorium service in Bangor.

I've only praise for our canon here, Emlyn Williams. He was so good with us as a family throughout Arfon's illness and he gave a very moving eulogy for Arfon at the service as well. Even so, we felt that we had suffered a double blow in a way. We had lost a son, brother, father and uncle, and we also felt that the farewell service had been such a damp squib with so few people allowed to be there. But then, thousands of other families had to endure exactly the same experience during this period because of the Covid rules.

It would have been very easy for us all to be overcome by despair and grief at this stage, but we had another cause to focus on and that was a help for us somehow in being able to look forward. It might come across as being hard-hearted to some, but it was a blessing to be able to set our minds on a positive cause after the intense sadness of losing Arfon. And we were very soon thrown back into that whole process because things intensified from this point onwards with a flood of messages and phone calls from Neil Hudgell in preparation for the case.

All the documentation had to be sent in to the Court of Appeal months before the hearings themselves in March 2021, so, as you can imagine, we were kept very busy for the rest of 2020 in helping Neil gather everything together. Time flew by and, before we knew it, we had arrived at Friday 23rd April 2021, the date that the Law Lords were to deliver their judgement in the Court of Appeal. We travelled down to London on the 6am early morning train to be at the court by 10.30am. It was such a bizarre experience to arrive in a London that was so closed-down and quiet, with none of the usual hustle and bustle you find in the city. We then met up with Neil Hudgell and Tim Maloney, the barrister who was representing us in the case. I remember I was very nervous and anxious and Neil telling me: "Don't worry, Noel. You're going to be all right. We've done all the work. It's in the bag, trust me."

Mind you, I'm sure that both Neil and Tim had some reason to feel nervous themselves that morning as they hadn't received a copy of the Law Lords' decision, which is usually delivered to the legal teams the night before the judgement itself. So, in a way, we were all going into the court completely in the dark that morning.

The thirty-three sub-postmasters whose cases were to be judged had been divided into three or four groups by the court, with the judgement then livestreamed to the different groups in various locations in the court. As it happens, I was lucky enough to be in the group in the court where the Law Lords themselves were sitting – two men and a woman. In the spotlight, for sure.

The opening words of one of the Law Lords struck absolute fear into my heart and sent me into the same kind of cold sweat I had experienced back in Caernarfon County Court all those years previously. "There are three ex sub-postmasters whose cases I dismiss at the very start," he announced in a very serious tone of voice.

"Oh, here we go again," I said to myself. "Am I going to be punished yet again, right at the end? Am I fated to be one of the unlucky ones in life?"

But then he began to read out the names of those he was clearing and my name was one of the first ones he mentioned. What can I say about that moment? The end of sixteen years of mental anguish, shame, darkness, hopelessness and losses of all sorts. Everything lifted and released in an instant in a few words from the Law Lord.

I've always put my trust in the Lord in life, whatever happens, and wasn't it oh so very apt that it was a Law Lord who was now delivering me from all the pain and loss I had suffered for so many years. I don't remember much more than that really. What else was there to listen to after hearing such life-changing words? I think the Law Lord then provided a short summary of the case, saying that a full judgement would be released around half an hour later.

I remember stumbling out of the court into the bright April sunlight, only to be faced with a massive media scrum all around and cameras flashing constantly. The next thing I knew, a journalist from the *Daily Mail* stuffed a microphone under my nose, asking: "How do you feel today?"

"The sun is shining and I am a free man," I said, trying my best to keep all my emotions in check. A very difficult task for this emotional man, I can tell you.

Sian and Edwin were at the opposite end of the media scrum at this point, but Sian, in her own special way, was able to clear them all out of the way, shouting at them at the top of her voice: "He's my father! Get out of my bloody way!"

We had a very special group hug after they eventually made their way to my side. The tears flowed between us like never before for several minutes. Because of all this emotion, I had clean forgotten all about going back into the court to receive the Law Lords' decision, but somebody else nipped back inside to get the judgement for me. This victory for us as a family called for a celebratory pint, but, of course, there were no pubs open because of Covid, so we decided to make our way back to Euston for the journey back to Ynys Môn.

There I was on the train, holding onto the judgement for dear life, reading it time and time again as we made the long journey home, telling myself: "Yes, Noel, it's down in black and white now. They have cleared my name at last. After all that struggle for so many years, I'm a free man again. The nightmare is finally over. For both myself and my family."

When we finally got back home to Gaerwen, the phone rang continually for hours and hours with so many well-wishers wanting to talk to me after the good news. I slept very well that night and awoke in the morning knowing that a sixteen-year-old nightmare was finally over. The stain on my character and my good name had been cleared at last. And everything could start again anew for me. Life begins at seventy-four!

Sian

Losing Arfon in 2020 was a heart-breaking experience for all of us as a family. We only had nine weeks with him from his diagnosis to his passing away. I still don't know how I came through that time, to be honest with you.

As I said earlier, the work at the nursing home through the Covid period was tough, as well as acting as the 'home secretary' for Dad's case during my evenings after work. And on top of all that, having to deal with seeing my own brother, Arfon, dying in front of me after this cruel illness came upon him. It was a horrible experience to watch him deteriorating on a daily basis, with none of us able to do anything to stop this slow slide towards death. It was such a tragic time for Mam and Dad in particular, of course, to see this happening to their eldest child. At a time that should have been so joyous for them with the clearing of Dad's name after so long, they had now been plunged back into a pit of despair and darkness. It was awful as well for Jade, Arfon's daughter who lived in Colwyn Bay and his ex-wife, Trish, who had remained on good terms with my brother despite the divorce.

During his time of radiotherapy treatments, Arfon had been a patient at Ysbyty Glan Clwyd, down the coast from Ynys Môn, but in his last days he was at Ysbyty Gwynedd in Bangor, closer to home. He also spent some time at home as well and I did my level best to care for him and make sure that he took all his medication – around twenty tablets in all – and so on.

He was my elder brother. I loved him and I wanted to do all I could for him in the time he had left. I remember Arfon asking me at one point how I was able to cope with all the work of caring for him and I turned round to him, saying, "Look, Arfon, I know you would do exactly the same for me if the roles were reversed and if I were the one who was ill, so I don't want any more questions like that!" He didn't respond, but I could see on his face that he understood and appreciated the point I was trying to make.

Of course, we all knew the score. Arfon had been given a very dark and final diagnosis right from the off by the doctors in Ysbyty Gwynedd, after the stage four cancer had been found. We knew instinctively that we only had a short time left with Arfon, so we wanted to make the best of the time we had left with him. It was a devastating period all round. We were in the middle of Covid and the lockdowns and all that, with a surreal feeling to everything that was going on all around us. I know that many others felt this feeling of complete unreality, but we knew that what was happening to Arfon was very, very real. In a way, we were saying goodbye to him every single day, but the end finally came for my brother on 26th March 2020.

I received a phone call at home telling me to come to the hospital as Arfon was weakening quickly. By the time I reached the ward, he had left us. All I could do was to go outside to steel myself for that drive home to break the news to Mam and Dad. I couldn't just phone them with news like this. I made the drive home with a jumble of emotions piling up inside me. I got out of the car and broke down in a flood of tears sitting on the wall outside the house.

Breaking that news to Mam and Dad was by far the hardest thing I've ever had to do in my whole life. Seeing their faces and their reactions to the news was heart-breaking. It was a complete nightmare to deal with. I've got to say that local people in the village and beyond were incredibly kind and caring when the news about Arfon filtered out. The phone kept ringing day and night, hundreds of cards came through the letter box, with people leaving gifts and other items on our front doorstep.

The value of community on Ynys Môn and people's bonds to each other really made its presence felt so, so strongly at that time. It definitely gave us some strength from somewhere to be able to deal with the loss. As a family, we had to wait ten days for the service at the crematorium in Bangor with some real doubts at one stage as to whether we could attend the service at all.

One of the directors of the local funeral directors, Rose and Thistle, had to break this news to me one morning over the phone. "I'm not sure whether you can go to the crematorium at all, Sian, with the Covid numbers rising again locally," said Gwenan, the lady in question.

Well, you can imagine the amount of stress and anxiety this created on top of everything else. Was there going to be an end to all this torture? But on the day, eighteen of us were allowed to attend the funeral at the crematorium. A number of Arfon's friends and acquaintances lined the road from Rhos Ellen as we left for the crematorium. This touched all of us, I can tell you.

Emlyn, our canon, did his level best under the circumstances, but the whole occasion was such a cold and uninvolving experience for us all, with everybody sitting apart in 'bubbles', which were imposed on us at the time.

During the service, I made a promise to Arfon that he would remain a key part of the process of clearing Dad's name, whatever happened. And that he would be a part of the celebrations, whenever those were to arrive. This happened by carrying Arfon's rucksack on my back when we went down to London for the Law Lords judgement a year later.

The next few months was a strange period for us all. Grieving Arfon and missing him every single day, but also looking forward to the day that Dad would finally be vindicated in the eyes of the world. A mixture of sadness and excitement, and the two feelings coming and going like waves breaking over me at different times. It was so difficult to manage these emotions – almost impossible at times – but then it's odd that whatever life throws at you, one can find a way somehow. This is exactly what happened this time, as well.

The big day finally arrived and we travelled down to London on the early train on a very bright day on April 23rd 2021. There was Dad, myself and Edwin, along with Lorraine Williams, a postmistress in a nearby village who had been through a similar process to Dad, although she hadn't been jailed, along with her daughter, Cameron.

When we arrived at the Court of Appeal, barriers had been erected across the entrance to the court and all the families had to stand across the road. The worse part of it all was to have to stand there in the crowd, no knowing what was actually going on in the court. And even when Dad emerged at 11am, we had no idea what was going on! We could see he was in tears, but were these tears of joy or tears of despair? After all we had been through, this extra delay seemed to be so, so cruel.

It was only several minutes later, after we fought our way through the huge media scrum all around us, that we were able to find out for ourselves. There's a picture of me whispering into Dad's ear: "What's happened, Dad?" I asked him. "I'm a free man, Sian," was his simple answer, before he was swallowed up by a large number of different media organisations who wanted to interview him about the judgement.

After what appeared to be an eternity, we were finally reunited with him and were able to make that train journey home to Ynys

Môn. What a happy and joyous trip that was. I still bring that journey to mind from time to time. It's still a very therapeutic memory for me. The release, the relief, the recognition that the long-lasting tragedy was over for us all now.

All those tears, those sleepless nights, all those endless nights on the computer trying to piece things together, the lack of any social life… it had all been worth it.

However, even after two court wins under our belts – in 2019 and now in 2021 – the battle was still not at an end because the next step had to be taken. Securing compensation for Dad after everything that had happened to him. And surprise, surprise, after all the twists and turns of the journey and all the time it had taken for us to get to this point, there was still a long and windy road to be travelled. And Sian Thomas had to keep her battle gear on to fight for Dad again. But that's another story.

The Local Response

There was an overwhelming response to the news of the Court of Appeal judgement locally. It was as if the whole of Ynys Môn wanted to be part of this victory for one of its own sons, showing yet again the community spirit and community mindedness that is still so strong here.

Here are some of the messages left on Sian's Facebook page over the following days:

- "Such good news for those who have suffered. Hell and prison for some of them."
- "Excellent news, Noel. I cried when I heard the news. What happened to you was such an appalling injustice. Large corporations totally devoid of morality. I knew from the very start that you were innocent." Councillor Arfon Wyn.
- "I've just heard about this fantastic news: warm regards to your Dad and a huge hug from me, brilliant for all the others cleared as well." Carys Jones.

- "So pleased that this mental torture has come to an end for you at long last Noel. We are overjoyed for you." Edward Morus Jones.
- "Oh Sian! I've cried and cried so much after seeing your Dad on the television. Give him a huge hug from me." Carys Wyn.
- "Great news – I've always thought the world of your Mam and Dad who gave me such a welcome in Gaerwen 34 years ago… Big hugs xxxxx." Rhian Watkin Owen.
- "Justice at long last." Sharon Jones-Williams.
- "Huge congratulations! Fantastic! But everyone who knew Noel knew he was innocent. It's an absolute scandal how this gentleman has been treated." Bleddyn Laslo Hughes.
- "Very good news Noel. I hope those people who were so quick to put you down will now be beating a path to your door to say sorry." Wil Thomas.
- "Brilliant. At last! I'm so pleased for you as it's been such a horrific time for you xx." Valmai Brown.
- "Very good news which is so heart-warming x." Rhian Owen Jones.
- "At last. This day has taken much too long to arrive. What a relief for everyone. Very good news." Jan Baller.
- "We always knew this day would come but the stress and heartache caused is immeasurable xx." Diane Varah.
- "So pleased to finally see justice prevail. Give your Dad a massive hug from me, my mum, Dad and Stephen. Well done on never giving up the fight xxx." Helen Scaife.
- "This has taken way too long. I'm delighted for you all, my heart bleeds for the horror you all went through, particularly your Dad xx". Sarah Williams-Davies.
- "Wonderful news Sian. At long last! Love to your Dad and all the family xx." Esme Williams.
- "Thank God but well overdue. What you have gone through as a family, I can only imagine xx." Elaine Holmes.

- "Always innocent. Never more of an honest man. Well done Noel." Gwen Evans.

The Muse of Môn

One of the extraordinary aspects of this case in the Appeal Court on 23rd April 2021 was the fact that the Westminster Government were also in front of their betters in a way, as it is the government, through their Business, Energy and Industrial Strategy Department (BEIS), who are the sole shareholder in Post Office Limited (POL).

In truth, POL, Fujitsu and the government were like some unholy trinity in the whole saga. And this intimate link between the three entities became even clearer to all when the public inquiry started at the end of 2020 was elevated to a statutory footing to become a full public inquiry in April 2021.

And this fine day on Friday 23rd April was the start of the process of bringing all of this to the light of day. After all the preparatory work that had been undertaken for the hearing, it took the Law Lords just half an hour to announce their judgement on that historic morning. This came in the form of a short oral summary, followed by a written judgement provided for all the claimants half an hour later.

These were the words of the Law Lords in adjudicating on the case of Noel Thomas. In considering the fact that he had been jailed for false accounting on the premise that he had accepted that Horizon worked perfectly, they said:

i) There was no justification for POL imposing such a condition before accepting Mr Thomas's plea.
ii) POL had dropped the theft charge and could no longer advance any case that he had stolen the money. That should have left the way open to Mr Thomas to suggest there was no actual loss and that he had only covered up a shortfall Horizon had created.
iii) An attendance note suggests that he was pressurised into accepting a positive position on Horizon as a condition for

POL dropping the theft charge and accepting a plea to false accounting.

iv) It is arguable that this exerted undue pressure on the appellant to accept that Horizon was 'working perfectly' before POL would be prepared to drop the theft which had the effect of imposing this agreement on him as a prior condition to dropping theft and taking the pleas to the alternative charge.

The Law Lords' main conclusion was that POL had failed in a very serious way to fulfil their basic duties in prosecuting SPMs on the basis of Horizon, thereby preventing every sub-postmaster from having a fair hearing in every single court where these charges were heard. This was summarised in this memorable line: "The failures of investigation and disclosure were in our judgement so egregious as to make the prosecutions of any of the 'Horizon cases' an affront to the conscience of the court."

Despite the fact that their judgement had depended heavily on Mr Justice Fraser's 'Common Issues' declaration in 2019, new evidence had also come to light by this stage and was mentioned by them in their judgement. Some of this new evidence was to be assessed yet further in the public inquiry to start later in 2021.

One of the most striking pieces of fresh evidence came after a Freedom of Information request by campaigner Eleanor Sheikh brought 'The Swift Review' to light – a damning report prepared for POL in 2016 by a barrister by the name of Jonathan Swift.

BIS (the government's Business and Technology Department at the time) had told the PO Chair at the time, Tim Parker, to commission this report, with Jonathan Swift briefed to assess how the Post Office had dealt with the complaints about Horizon. In his report, Swift wrote there were grounds for serious concerns about the quality of the evidence used to prosecute the sub-postmasters and serious concerns concerning some of the tactics used by POL. He said: "The allegation that POL has effectively bullied SPMs into pleading guilty to offences by unjustifiably overloading the charge sheet is a stain on the character of the business."

The public inquiry under the chairmanship of Sir Wyn Williams was also to hear a raft of incredible new revelations during 2022 and 2023. It became apparent that the Post Office board had initially refused to approve the process of introducing the Horizon system to the Post Office in September 1999, raising their concerns about 'training, the stability of the system itself and the quality of its data'. Only for this decision to be overturned completely just a month later in October 1999.

One of Horizon's Programme Directors, David Miller, apologised to the inquiry for his statement that the system was 'robust' and 'fit for purpose', stating that it had never been those things from the very start.

Damning evidence was also presented by a development manager by the name of Dave McDonnell, the joint author of a report that had warned about problems with Horizon back in 1998, before its introduction into Post Offices all over the UK. McDonnell noted there was a 'wild west' mentality among those who were developing EPOS – the computer programme for Horizon – with no standards, no structure and no discipline in place. He further stated that the code developed for the system was among the very worst he had ever come across in his professional career.

And we then had the Ismay Report, an internal report for the Post Office in 2010, which was finally revealed into the public domain for the very first time. In this report, the author – a senior manager within the Post Office – urged the Post Office not to investigate any complaints about the failing of the Horizon system lest it lead to opening the floodgates completely – having to consider complaints from the past and potential complaints in the future, too. This one report effectively extended the torture endured by Noel Thomas and other postmasters for another ten cruel years.

Some other incredible revelations have come to light over the last couple of months at the inquiry as well. Another piece of detective work by Eleanor Sheikh, this time at the National Archives, revealed a briefing note sent to PM Tony Blair in December 1998.

In this briefing note, Geoff Mulgan of No 10's Policy Unit alerted Blair to 'what many see as a flawed (Horizon) system'. Along with a handwritten response from Blair himself: 'I would favour option 1 but for Geoff's statement that the system itself is flawed'.

We then heard that the charges against one sub-postmistress (Julie Wolstenhome) were dropped by the Post Office back in 2003 after they were told by an IT expert that the Horizon system was completely flawed. The expert then refused to change his story despite pressure from the PO to do so. The postmistress in question eventually signed a non-disclosure agreement to bring that particular case to an end.

But even with this damning information received so early in the process, the Post Office continued to prosecute other sub-postmasters for a further ten years on the very same basis – i.e. the flawed Horizon system.

There was also the last-minute 'no show' of Gareth Jenkins, a Fujitsu engineer whose evidence was used to jail so many sub-postmasters, including Noel Thomas. This was down to the fact that the Post Office contacted the inquiry at 10.30pm, the evening before Jenkins was due to appear, to say that nearly 5,000 documents relating to Jenkins's role in the saga could not be properly considered. The documents concerned had been disclosed, but the inquiry team were unable to read them in the time available to them.

This prompted the inquiry chair, Sir Wyn Williams, to invoke a 2005 Criminal Inquiries Act (Section 21) warning that any future failures to disclose evidence by the Post Office 'carries a threat of criminal sanctions' (including a sentence of up to fifty-one weeks' imprisonment).

As this book goes to press, some more of the higher level officers within both the Post Office and Fujitsu are likely to be called in front of the inquiry, with even some whisperings that senior politicians will also be summoned in due course. It would be supremely ironic if this whole saga finished by going back to the very start. By calling a former UK prime minister and asking him why he insisted on introducing a known faulty computer system, which would cause so much pain and suffering, and personal and financial losses for hundreds of sub-postmasters for so many years.

More generally, it is for the public inquiry to ask why each successive government representative from 2000 onwards failed so disastrously in their duty to oversee the Post Office, given it is a company solely owned by the government; given its weighty social purpose and its importance to communities across the four nations; and given their neglect has facilitated a cover-up at the Post Office that has lasted far longer than it might have done, ruining hundreds of sub-postmasters' lives and delaying justice.

And with some even questioning whether there will ever be a suitably transparent and truthful response by a UK Government to this travesty of justice, other avenues may well now have to be explored. On the eve of publication of this book, Alan Bates, the spokesperson for the Sub-Postmasters Alliance announced he was now considering civil proceedings against Post Office Executives, after what he termed "20 years of no consequences" for their actions.

Noel Thomas has always been fulsome in his praise for Alan Bates as the inspiration and driving force of the sub-postmasters' long and drawn-out campaign for justice. And it would be very fitting if he would also prove to be the figure-head for the next stage in ensuring the final resolution of the whole saga.

And finally

In bringing this modern morality tale to a close, it's only right to acknowledge the role played by many outstanding journalists to bring this to light over the past decade or so, and who have managed to move things forwards for all of the affected sub-postmasters. Individuals such as Nick Wallis, Karl Flinders and Tom Witherow, who have dedicated years of their lives to the story and who have performed such an outstanding example of public interest in doing so.

The growth of the importance of social media has also been a key component more recently, with many ordinary citizens contributing to the process of raising public awareness about the whole saga. One of the most prominent of these is Eleanor Shaikh, who has a family connection here in North West Wales and who, as part of her investigations, has also become a good friend of the Thomas family over recent years. Eleanor has managed to unearth a huge amount of new information about the Post Office scandal by means of Freedom of Information requests, earning an honourable mention for all her work by a leading barrister in the public inquiry.

But for all her doggedness in bringing to light some of the key details that the Post Office, Fujitsu and three governments wanted to conceal, it's the personal story of Noel and his family that has most motivated Eleanor. Describing him as a 'gentle giant', Eleanor first met Noel in 2019 at the garden centre in Ynys Môn, immediately taken by his rich Welsh accent – "rugged as the mountains of Eryri that loom over the island of his birth". Noel told her he could write a book about what he'd gone through – and he certainly wasn't wrong about that!

"Who could have imagined that four years on, despite the subpostmasters' resounding victory at the High Court, Noel would still be fighting for a settlement sizeable enough to reflect the suffering that he and his family have endured?" Eleanor told me.

"I sincerely hope that now as I did four years ago that Noel can start living his life without the shadow of the Post Office's brutality hanging over his every move. But sometimes 'hope' isn't enough. Sometimes it isn't enough to respond with wishful thinking, with kind words or just silence. It isn't enough to assume that others will fight the sub-postmasters' corner or to believe that their persecutors will voluntarily right their wrongs. Sometimes a stand has to be taken, because we simply can't ignore the scale of suffering or the wider implications of this devastating scandal.

We can't be hoodwinked by a political indifference, which has sought to heal unimaginable wounds with half-hearted compensation settlements and plaster apologies of 'lessons learned'. We can't let our vigilance slip and allow the burden of proof to be reversed as it was for two decades plus by a rogue state-owned prosecutor.

Whatever our walk of life, whatever we can contribute, we owe it to those who have dedicated their lives to serving our communities to reach out in solidarity, to lend our voices and our strength to those whose lives are still ensnared in the 'greatest miscarriage of our lifetime'. For their struggle goes on and it goes deeper and higher than most of us imagine because it reaches to the very heart of what we consider to be just and civilised.

As Noel himself has reminded me, "It's one for all and all for one."

We'll finish *The Stamp of Innocence* by honouring the father-and-daughter bond that has shone through the whole saga for so many years and ask the two of them, Noel and Sian, to sum up their latest thoughts in late September 2023 about the whole saga.

Sian

The inquiry – for all of Sir Wyn's valiant efforts – is just extending our frustration. We are seeing the Post Office playing the same old game of delay, deflection and denial. It's two years since Dad's name was cleared by the Court of Appeal and we are yet to receive our full compensation. And there's still no real sense that they are owning this and making things right. No one is willing to take responsibility and show the kind of contrition we need to see. And they still make us jump through so many hoops to actually receive the compensation that is due to us. And the question I keep coming back to time and time again is this: when, oh when, will someone actually be brought to justice for what was been done to Dad and countless other innocent people?

On a more positive note, we have been blown away as a family by the warmth and love and support we have received from people on Ynys Môn – especially since the publication of *Llythyr Noel* – the Welsh language book – published back in April. It's amazing how many times each week I'm stopped in the street by people who tell me they've read the book. They feel embarrassed to say they 'enjoyed' reading it, but what they are trying to say is that it has moved them and touched them in a big way. I think the book has also had a wider impact as it has boosted the Welsh language on the island, in my view.

The language has been under a lot of pressure here over recent years with lack of employment opportunities and young people moving away, and English becoming so powerful through media/social media – and maybe a sense as well that the language is not so relevant now. But being able to tell this story in Welsh first has given people a lot of confidence in the language again – that it is a medium to tell such a powerful, modern-day story. A language that can move people, shake people, inspire people again. So that's been great to see and a huge boost for the Ynys Môn identity in general.

***

At the start of the book, we remember how Noel Thomas felt that he had been thrown defenceless into the lion's den in the prison at Walton. In the book of Daniel (from where the phrase 'the lion's den' comes), there are four beasts mentioned, representing four different oppressive empires: Babylon, Persia, Greece and Rome. All described as monsters, oppressing the people and having authority over people for a certain time, before passing away in turn.

And in this modern tale, there have also been four beasts who have acted as these oppressors. The Post Office, Fujitsu, Government and Whitehall. The first three beasts are very clear in people's minds, but perhaps the fourth beast, Whitehall, is not so clear for people. The machine in the background that obfuscates, delays and deflects everything has played a big hand in all the proceedings. It's also intriguing that a courtroom scene is described in the Book of Daniel where the four beasts are finally brought to justice, since so many are now anticipating that justice will also be served on the modern beasts in a modern-day courtroom once the public inquiry has finished its work.

But just as Daniel's faith saw him through all his trials and tribulations, faith has also delivered Noel in exactly the same way as he used to deliver all those letters across his island for so many years – with his frequent visits to his favourite church, Tal y Llyn, being a wider metaphor for the spiritual strength he needed to overcome the trials and tribulations of this world.

Noel

Small churches like Tal y Llyn are stamped all over Ynys Môn and they are all very special in their own ways, of course, and such an important part of our heritage and history as a people. In a way, of course, I've also been stamped by the experiences I've been through with all this. It's been a long and difficult journey for sure, but I've survived and I think I've become a more resilient person as well. I haven't lost my faith in humanity, for all that's happened. If anything, the support and warmth I've received from my fellow Monwysion (islanders) has restored my faith in humanity. And deepened my love for Ynys Môn and its people. A special place and a special people.

Many a time, I've been at Tal Llyn looking at the mountains, looking over the church and thinking of Psalm 121 – the mountains protecting Ynys Môn and the spirit protecting me as well. I can only say the opening lines of the Psalm in Cymraeg – the language of heaven itself, of course:

'*Dyrchafaf fy llygaid i'r mynyddoedd, o ble daw fy nghymorth?*
Fy nghymorth a ddaw oddi wrth yr Arglwydd
Yr hwn a greodd Nefoedd a Daear.'

A simple faith. A grounded faith. A trusting faith. It's all so ironic when one considers the fact that one of the main protagonists in the Post Office saga – one of Noel's chief persecutors, in a way – was also an ordained vicar with the Church of England, in the form of Paula Vennells, Post Office Chief Executive between 2012 and 2019, who was later awarded a CBE for her 'services' to the Post Office and was paid no less than £700,000 in the job in 2018/19, including bonuses for 'achieving commercial sustainability and profitability'.

Her period in the post was the obfuscation stage, where the Post Office was desperately denying there was anything amiss with their IT systems and that no convicted sub-postmaster had been unjustly treated. This façade was exposed by Judge Fraser at the 2019 High Court Judgement, saying that the Post Office's words – for whom Paula Vennells was the figurehead – boiled down to "bare assertions and denials that ignore what has actually occurred and amounts to the 21st century equivalent of maintaining that the earth is flat."

If ever there was a contrast between a faith lived and a faith simply 'professed' – between a daily belief that shapes life's decisions compared to a belief that is worn as Sunday best, only to be discarded on weekdays in the harsh reality of the corporate world – the case of Noel Thomas versus Paula Vennells seems to sum it all up.

One cannot escape the deep irony that Paula Vennells claimed to take biblical inspiration from King Solomon for her role as Post Office Chief Executive, "who showed humility in asking for a wise and understanding heart so he could rule his people with justice"(1 Kings 3).

With Paula Vennells expected to be among the senior management summoned before the public inquiry in the next stage, the 'target the head' strategy we mentioned in the very first chapter might well come into play again – centuries down the line. In a wider sense as well, the Noel Thomas versus Paula Vennells story is a striking metaphor for the growing realisation concerning the complete mismatch between the experiences of ordinary people and a privileged class in the UK today, for whom accountability, honesty and truth seems to be a very alien concept.

The whole saga seems to symbolise a broken Britain where the trust between people and the institutions that are supposed to represent them is completely destroyed – as well as the Post Office, add mainstream media, political parties and politicians, the church, the medical profession, the banking system, the education system and many more such institutions. Perhaps this is one of the reasons that the story has resonated so much with the public. Not just on Ynys Môn and Wales, but throughout the UK as well.

The Stamp of Innocence started by declaring that the island identity was a key part of this whole story about the trials and tribulations that came the way of one ordinary Welsh sub-postmaster. And we'll finish with the island as well.

At the launch of the Welsh-language book *Llythyr Noel* in April, the leader of Ynys Môn County Council, Llinos Medi asked this very important question: "What can we learn as an island community from this scandal?"

Noel Thomas's words in response that night still ring true: "We have to keep fighting – that's the only answer. To not give up, but to keep fighting for our future here. To keep our spirit alive on Ynys Môn and to support and sustain each other."

And the people said, "Amen."

Appendix

Here we include the names of all those individuals who were kind enough to contribute to a Crowdfunder to finance the writing of this book. The Crowdfunder raised £9,207.

Gwyn Wigley Evans

Elizabeth Downs

Elliot Griffiths

Sarah Ruddock

George Canty

Gill Grain

Jenny Linford

Victoria Strachan

Pam Parry

Peter Thomas

Kevin Fitzsimons

Bethan Edwards

Eifion Jones

Gwenda Thomas

Mrs J M Sims

Sarah Jane Chaloner

Michael John Hind

John White

Joanne Norman

Ish Thomson

Margery Lorraine Williams

Andrew Walker

Mrs G L Augustine

Lesley N John

Mary Weber

Adam Salem

PS Everard

Carol Williams

Gillian Howard

Susan Craddock

Penelope Williams

Paul Gilbert

Charles Elliot

Janet Downie

Paul Marshall
Ian Fagelson
John Tobin
Kathleen Hassani
Timothy Brentnall
Jade Bowyer
Alex Toft
Chester's Mun
Andrew Curry
Robert Nicholson
Leigh Sparks
Nick Payne
Martin Davies
Douglas Buffrey
Pam Martin
Brent Jay
David Williams
Alison Evans
Varchas Patel
Aileen Murphie
Ian Warren
Nichola Arch
Jon Robinson
Mark Baker
Pattie Abee Jenkins
Janet Rogers
Peter Davies
Danny Houston
Sandra Tizzard
Eileen Read
Andy Fordham
Nehal Parmar
Alan Fraser and Miranda
Ingram

Roger Symes
Sean Hudson
Thomas Ward
Chris Lidyard
Sian Pearce
Andrew Neville
R Moorhead
Nigel P Pentland
Rosemary Brocklehurst
Julie Beisner
George Peacock
Richard Roll
Martin Gray
Nigel M Derby
John O'Sullivan
Geoff Crouch
Jackie Bridger
Hilary Lesley Jones
Gail Ward
Amanda Fairclough
B A Wright
Liz Walters
Edward Bainston
Carol Charlton
Manxstar
William Arthur Hogg
Shane Johnson
Jeff Hawkins
Margaret Scott
Morella Swallow
Robert Furber
Karola Zakrzewska
David Rooke
Christopher Read

Andrew Neale
Piers Pettman
Richard Smith
Jeremy Thomas
Padre
Nick Frank
Angela Mollison
Kay Feltham-Jones
Ronald J Warmington
Nicol McGregor
Julia Van Coevorden
Barbara Turner
Graham Harrison
Stewart Ware
A R Collins
Bilbocraft
Hugh Cooper
Ruth Bender
Wendy Percival
Richard Wong
Paul Green
Joanne Foulger
Iain King
John Baxter McLaughlin

Colin Byrne
Robert Stokes
Jeremy Folkes
Tim Chapman
H Smal
Roger Winter
Sue Rees
Allyce Hibbert
Nick Wallis
Laurence Williams
Owain Lorenz Pennar
Dr. Dafydd Rees
Sue Soper
Alicia Clegg
Huw Davies
Ian Henderson
Mcquire Jones
Brian Whelton
El Shaikh
William Griffiths
Angela Taylor
Carol
Dafydd Williams